SIMPLY
SPEAKING

OTHER BOOKS BY PEGGY NOONAN

What I Saw at the Revolution

Life, Liberty and the Pursuit of Happiness

SIMPLY SPEAKING

HOW TO COMMUNICATE YOUR IDEAS
WITH STYLE, SUBSTANCE, AND CLARITY

PEGGY NOONAN

ReganBooks
An Imprint of HarperCollins*Publishers*

Grateful acknowledgment is made for permission to reprint from the following:

Five Secrets of Speaking the Language of Leadership by James C. Humes. Copyright © 1991 by James C. Humes. Reprinted by permission of William Morrow & Co.

Great Speeches in History, Revised Edition by William Safire, ed. Copyright © 1992, 1997 by The Cobbett Corporation. Reprinted by permission of W. W. Norton & Company, Inc.

Grateful acknowledgment is made to Peter G. Peterson for permission to use his speech honoring Liz Smith.

HarperCollins books may be purchased for educational, business, or sales promotional use. For information please write: Special Markets Department, HarperCollins Publishers, Inc., 10 East 53rd Street, New York, NY 10022.

FIRST EDITION

Designed by Kris Tobiassen

Library of Congress Cataloging-in-Publication Data

Noonan, Peggy, 1950–
    Simply speaking : how to communicate your ideas with style, substance, and clarity / Peggy Noonan. — 1st ed.
        p. cm.
     ISBN 0-06-039212-6
     1. Public speaking. I. Title.
PN4121.N66   1998
808.5'1—dc21   97-32537

98 99 00 01 02 ❖/RRD 10 9 8 7 6 5 4 3

For Joan and Pete

The mind is a wonderful thing. It starts working the minute you're born and never stops until you get up to speak in public.

—ROSCOE DRUMMOND

ACKNOWLEDGMENTS

All books are pushed into being by little platoons. For their inspiration and information, warm thanks to Art Buchwald, Ben Elliott, Tiffany Ericksen, Joni Evans, Slade Gorton, Lisa Johnston, Genevieve Kopel, Jim Pinkerton, Lauren Pollack, Lisa Schiffren, Lisa Schwarzbaum, Diane Salvatore, Miranda Tollman, and Kerry Tymchuk. At ReganBooks, special thanks to Jeremie Ruby-Strauss for his patience and leadership, John Ekisian for his command and good humor, and Judith Regan for her warmth, wit, and boldness; also for not backing down on the pink satin gown.

INTRODUCTION

This is a book of advice and anecdotes about the writing and giving of speeches. It is about what works and what doesn't when you're communicating using only words in the air.

It is not solely about political speeches, for they are only one stream off the great river of rhetoric. Instead it is for people in any area of life who find themselves asked to speak in public and are not entirely comfortable with the prospect.

Which would be a lot of us. We are all asked sooner or later to say a few words at the annual meeting, the parent-teacher gathering, the awards dinner, the memorial service, the wedding. But I think these days Americans are speaking in public more than ever. For years social observers have worried that TV, videos and home entertainment centers were detaching us from each other, fracturing our sense of community, keeping us home on the couch watching instead of outside with others doing. But I am increasingly struck by the sheer number of meetings and gatherings that take place every night in America's cities and towns—lectures, visiting authors, visiting celebrities, "An Evening with . . . ," cultural gatherings, political meetings. People seem to be speechifying more than ever.

The changes that have swept modern business have contributed to the talking boom. As more and more businesses become involved in the new media technologies, as we become a nation of fewer widgets and more Web sites, a new premium has been put on the oldest form of communication: the ability to stand and say what you think in front of others. At the business conference, in the teleconference and the seminar, businessmen and -women are increasingly called on to speak about their industry, their plans, the realities within which they operate, what government is doing or not doing to make things better or worse. And they're not alone: Teachers and professors and reporters and doctors are out there too. Sooner or later we're all on C-Span. Postmodern America is becoming what it was a hundred years ago: a big Chautauqua Circuit where everyone goes to listen or talk.

In one way this is nothing new. The first word of the first caveman may have been *hello,* but it was probably followed by stand-up: "So I'm sitting by the fire and this antelope comes over the hill—" (I suspect the first punctuation was not the period but the colon.) But now the audience is bigger, the event is being broadcast, and a certain ease is expected.

The astonishing thing is that people have grown so good at it, so capable of meeting the demands of their public moment. It seems that all of us, from the slowest teenager in the poorest tenement, know how to appear on television—how to act and move our hands and voices on talk shows, on Sally Jessy and Montel. We know how to speak to the local camera crew at the scene of the story. No one is shy anymore. We are like a nation of little anchormen and -women, giving the reporter the sentence she needs, shaking our heads in the right way. We are media savvy. But we still, being human, have trouble saying things that are true and interesting. Instead we tend to say what we know is expected.

The exception to all this surprising and arguably depressing media expertise—technology, after all, was supposed to help us make communication simpler and clearer, not just more prevalent—is the speech. A speech is more formal, more focused—the audience is not distracted by the story unfolding around you; there is no host to ask, "And how did you feel at that moment?" Because everyone knows you had time to prepare, and have presumably done your best, that is what people expect: your best. You stand at the podium alone, clear your throat, look out at the eager faces looking at you . . .

There was a poll a few years ago that said that of all the things to be feared in life—death, disease, drowning—Americans picked as their number-one fear . . . public speaking. I was not surprised. I had been a public-speaking-phobe for forty years when I made my first speech.

But stage fright is only half the challenge for most people. The other half is the Now I Have to Write It problem. Which means: You have to figure out what you're going to say, and then you have to figure out how you're going to say it. Here your mind freezes, held back by a number of things, including the idea many people have, the idea they've received, that speeches are magic, that they are some combination of sorcery and show business that cannot, by a normal human, be achieved.

But speeches are not magic. Reduced to its essentials, a speech is a combination of information and opinion written on paper and spoken with the mouth. If you can have a thoughtful conversation you can probably write and give a thoughtful speech.

This book is intended to offer information and observations that will help.

*   *   *

When I told a friend that I was writing this book, she said, "How can you teach someone to write a speech when it's such an intuitive sort of thing?" It is. But my thinking is, there are things in every art or craft that can be pointed out and emphasized, pitfalls that can be highlighted and avoided. If I were a piano teacher I would tell my pupil, "I can't make you Toscanini, only you and God can make you Toscanini. But I can tell you things I've learned, and you may benefit from my experience."

These are things I've learned.

AND SO
WE BEGIN

CHEER UP, EVERYONE'S HAD THEIR MOMENT

I'm tempted to begin this the way *Reader's Digest* used to: *So you want to give a speech . . .*

There you are in the den, the kitchen or the dining room, and you're thinking, How do I get out of it?

The original invitation probably left you almost limp with self-love. *They like me, they really like me.* But now it is three weeks later and the speech is Tuesday and your mouth is dry as cotton, your heart dysrhhythmic, and in its wild thumping you are hearing the words: *I gotta GIVE it, I GOT to stand there and they'll ALL be LOOKing at me . . .*

Your first thoughts are constructive alternatives: If I get in a car accident I won't have to speak. But it's hard to calibrate the exact extent of injury when you swerve across the fast lane into a divider, so you reconsider.

And sit. And shift in your chair. And begin, in a desultory manner, to type:

"Thank you, ladies and gentlemen. It is nice to be here."

Try a joke.

"Thank you, ladies and gentlemen. Before I get to the heart of my remarks, I just thought I'd tell you— There's three guys in a boat, a black guy, an Irishman and a Jew—"

No.

"A man walks into a bar with a duck on his head—"

No.

"So Bill Clinton's jogging down the street and he sees a cat in heat and he says—"

No.

"Thank you for being here. I mean of course you had to be here, but thank you for inviting me even though I of course had to be here too, but I didn't think I'd ever have to speak—"

No.

You try to summon from within what frightens you most. It is dishearteningly easy. You will be so nervous you will not be able to stop shaking and they will see your arms vibrate—you will look like a three-year-old saying, "See, Daddy, I can fly." You will vibrate so hard you'll knock the pages off the podium, you'll bend to pick them up, lose your place, look out at the audience and your first words will be "In conclusion . . . "

No. You can put your arms on the side of the podium, grip it with your hands. That'll fool everyone. You'll look commanding, like Clinton. But: You will lose your voice! You'll clear your throat and open your mouth and you'll make this little itty-bitty weak mouse sound—*eeep eeep eeep*—and they will know: You lost your voice from nerves.

They will know something they didn't know. In fact, they will know something you didn't know: You are afraid of them.

And how could you be? They are your clients, whom you fool every day! They are your friends! They are that dumb-as-a-stone teacher your daughter had two years ago! Afraid of them?

No, you're not, not individually. But in the aggregate—eight hundred eyes watching you, eight hundred feet ready to walk if you flop, four hundred brains waiting to be entertained, four hundred witnesses to the fact that deep down you are a frightened little *eeep-eeep*-going mouse.

Here's some good news. Right now you are in the worst part. The reality you are imagining is worse than the reality that will be. They used to say the coward dies a thousand deaths, the brave man but one, but maybe it's closer to the truth to say that people with a vivid imagination die a thousand deaths, dullards but one.

And a vivid imagination is a sign of intelligence.

And intelligent people can give speeches.

Also, there's this: Even your most important speech isn't that important. Life is long and full of minutes, that crucial speech you made three years ago turns out actually not to have been a destiny changer, but just another knot in the ribbon of your life.

So don't be so nervous. It's only talking. If you fail miserably, nothing changes. It will momentarily sadden your friends and hearten your enemies. But only momentarily. And you—you'll just have to try again until you get it right.

I write in terms of near-phobic fear because, as I said, that is what I once had, and I am projecting. I had a horrible experience when I was in seventh grade. Before that I could stand up in class and speak with ease and enjoyment, but one day in seventh-grade English class we were each called upon, row by row, to read aloud from "The Song of Hiawatha." When it got to my row I became fearful, not knowing why. When the student in front of me stood for her turn I became so frightened I broke out in sweat. When it was my turn I stood with the book in my hands, began to read—"And beyond them stood the forest / Stood the groves of singing pine-trees"—and within a stanza lost my voice. It began to shake, to weaken, and then it just stopped coming out of me. The teacher looked up. I think I said something like, "I'm sick." She told me to sit down. I did. With great embarrassment and confusion.

Years later I would realize I had had an anxiety attack. But I didn't know that then, and what happened when I couldn't read the poem so took the wind from my sails, so traumatized me . . . that I never stood to speak in public again until I was forty years old.

This kind of experience is not uncommon. I know a man who runs an important media business who suffers terribly before he gives a speech, who in fact for twenty years devoted considerable energy and ingenuity to successfully avoiding ever having to make one, because of something that happened to him when he was a little boy. He was in the first or second grade when they had a school play and he was assigned the part of a boy stuck in a box. At a certain point he was to spring from the box and say a sentence. But when the moment came he couldn't get out of the box, it wouldn't open, and when he finally forced his way out he stood up, looked at the audience . . . and started to cry. The audience, composed of parents and teachers who thought they had witnessed something human and comic—as they had, though of course it was also more than that, it was poignant and touching and sad—laughed. My friend never forgot the laughter, and never completely got over it.

A memory like that can follow you forever, can shape decisions you make as an adult. But when you have to get over it, when the facts of your current life force you to get over it, you do. My friend now makes speeches. He still throws up first, but he makes them.

*   *   *

The speech I made at forty was to a small audience in upstate New York. It had been arranged by my publishers, who had become alarmed when I told them that I would have trouble promoting my first book because I was afraid of public speaking and did not think I would be able to conquer my fear any time soon. But you must, said the publisher, you are legally obliged to speak about your work: It's in your contract.

Having to do it, I did it, agreeing to this "practice speech" they had arranged, to be given to an audience of about a hundred people whom I did not know and would never see again—exactly the kind of audience you want your first time out. These were the employees of a company that boosted morale by getting them together once a month to hear about how business was going, what's up at headquarters. My appearance was tacked on at the end, as, as they put it, a special treat. I still think, Those poor people.

I went up to the stage, stood at the little podium in the little auditorium, fiddled with the mike and began, comforted only by this thought: They can boo me but they can't kill me. If I fainted, lost my voice or burst into tears . . . well, at least I wouldn't die. Unlike Sir Thomas More, who, the last time he spoke in public, was then beheaded.

I had written out a text of presidential anecdotes. I liked them and thought they were interesting. I read them aloud. Very slowly. My plan was, if I lost my voice I'd just stand and breathe and then say one word. Then I'd stand and breathe again and force out another. As in, "Thank .... you."

I was not, as you can imagine, very good. But I didn't lose my voice. I may have sounded like a drugged person, but I spoke. And after fifteen minutes I stopped hearing my heart in my ears. At the end everyone was nice, and applauded, and said things like, "That was interesting." Which I chose to believe on the theory that if you never question insults you should never question compliments.

But what I remember most, the key thing, is that about halfway through the speech I improved, became more focused and more sure, because my mind fastened on what I was saying, *and I wanted to be understood.* The desire to be understood is the desire to connect, and wanting to connect made me look up at the audience now and then, and gesture, as people do in conversation.

I realized: When you forget yourself and your fear, when you get beyond self-consciousness because your mind is thinking about what you are trying to communicate, you become a better communicator.

That was my first lesson, a simple one but one that nobody had ever told me: Have a text that interests you. It will help you get beyond you, help you focus on your thoughts and not your presentation. This is the beginning of the end of self-consciousness, which is the beginning of the end of fear.

PRELIMINARIES

Put your anxiety about speaking aside now, and start thinking about writing. Here are three things to keep in mind as you begin.

NO SPEECH SHOULD LAST MORE THAN TWENTY MINUTES

Why? Because Ronald Reagan said so. Reagan used to say that no one wants to sit in an audience in respectful silence for longer than that, if that. He also knew twenty minutes is more than enough time to say the biggest, most important thing in the world. The Gettysburg Address went three minutes or so, the Sermon on the Mount hardly more. It is usually and paradoxically true that the more important the message, the less time required to say it.

I would add that forty years of the habit of television has probably affected how people receive information. They are used to fifteen- or eighteen-minute pieces on *60 Minutes* or *Prime Time Live.* They are used to twelve-minute segments within the arc of the drama on *ER* and *Homicide.* They are

used to commercials interrupting the flow of thought. They
are not used to watching forty- and fifty- and sixty-minute presentations without a break, and there is no reason to believe
they want to get used to it.

So keep in mind what Hubert Humphrey's wife is said to
have advised him: "Darling, for a speech to be immortal it
need not be interminable."

A twenty-minute speech is about ten typed pages long, double-spaced.

YES, YOU SHOULD WRITE OUT THE TEXT

You may know exactly what you want to say, it's all in your
head and all you have to do is reel it out. Fine. But you ought
to have a written text to fall back on if for some reason you
need it. Winston Churchill, in his middle years, as a member
of Parliament, once stood to speak on an important issue. All
eyes turned to him with expectation: He was Churchill, the
great orator. He was also exhausted, stressed, and possibly
hungover. He began to speak . . . and went blank. He looked
around, confused. He stood for a few moments saying nothing. Then he shuffled to his seat, appalled and embarrassed.
His enemies made much of it.

Churchill no doubt wished he'd had a text from which he
could have read while his mind regathered itself.

What happened to him happens to all. If you've ever gone
blank in the middle of a thought and forgotten what you were
talking about or what you were about to say, you have had
such a moment. Don't have it in public if you don't have to.

Experienced speakers often bring cards on which they've
written a point or a phrase or two. (Reagan did this for years,

before he was president; before each speech, when he was governor and when he was first running for president, he'd shuffle the cards and change the order of his points to keep things fresh not only for the audience but for himself.) Reading from cards is fine if you're a pro and it's second nature to you and you really have locked in your head exactly what the point and the phrase signify. But most of us aren't pros.

I have made more than a hundred speeches and I still can't do it from cards; every word has to be written out in a text I place on the lectern. Knowing that I have it to fall back on, I feel free to ad-lib and embellish, as one would with cards.

HUMOR IS ESSENTIAL

Every speech needs it and you need it too, probably at the top.

Ronald Reagan was a perfectionist about public speaking, and by the time I knew him he was a longtime veteran. But he was always nervous before he spoke. Good performers always are, because they're serious about what they're doing and want badly to do well. Reagan always needed a joke at the top of a speech because he needed the quick victory of laughter. It helped him relax. It also helped the audience relax. It's a speaker's way of saying, "This won't be painful, humor is allowed here." Also, during the laughter everyone in the audience sort of gets to shift around and get comfortable in their chairs.

But more important, humor is gracious and shows respect. It shows the audience you think enough of them to want to entertain them.

Before you begin to write a speech, get on the phone and tell your friends what you're doing and ask them if they have any suggestions for jokes or witticisms or funny references. If you get some right away and they're good it will boost your confidence and better your work: You've already laughed, and now you know you're going to make other people laugh when you tell them what you just heard.

But this process can take time, so you want to start it as soon as you start thinking about the speech.

An example: A year ago I was to make a speech before a political group in New York City. I knew what I wanted to say about politics but I couldn't think of anything that would make the audience laugh. So I called a friend of mine and said, "Help." He asked for the specifics of the event. It's a dinner, I said, at the Waldorf. About four hundred people, they're sophisticated, it's a fancy event. The mayor will be there, he speaks after me, I introduce him.

My friend went off to think. A few days later he called. "Did you see the picture of Giuliani at the press club thing the other night?" I had. Mayor Giuliani had taken part in a press club skit and had come out onto the stage in full drag—blond wig, big eyelashes, long beaded dress. The pictures were all over the papers, and they were particularly striking because Giuliani looked not so much amusing as real weird.

"This is the joke," said my friend. "You stand up there and say, 'It's wonderful to be in the Waldorf, in this lovely and elegant room. I was so excited by the prospect, and by seeing all of you, that I was going to get all decked out in a beautiful gown. But I didn't want to take the chance of showing up in the same thing the mayor might be wearing, so—'"

I used it and it got a big laugh. In part because an audience likes to see an important person get teased, it's a good leveler. This of course must be done good-naturedly. The Gridiron Club in Washington, which meets once a year to spoof politicians in skits, has a motto: "We singe but never burn." Take it as yours.

The Giuliani joke had a good one-month shelf life. A friend of mine who was to speak a week later at a formal fund-raiser in a New York hotel called to say "Help!" and I gave her the joke. Again it got a big laugh. And a few days later she gave it to another friend who was to speak, and on it went.

If you are naturally humorous and think of jokes on your own, great. But for most of us a little trolling helps. Everyone has a friend or two who's particularly funny or at least knows the latest jokes. (The latest one in New York, as I write, is: An Irishman, a rabbi, a Puerto Rican and a gay guy walk into a bar. The bartender looks at them and says, "What is this, a joke?" This would go over well at the Rotary, less well before a joint session of Congress.) When you ask for help, tell your friends the specifics of the event: where you're speaking, why you're speaking, what your subject is, who's in the audience. Think about the timing of the speech. Is the NCAA championship on TV at the same time? Then promise you'll be brief, refer to the game and say something about the famous coach who loses his temper or the ancestral rivalry between this team and that.

A Note on Humor to Women of a Certain Age

I have noticed over the years that women in business and politics often avoid two things when they speak. They tend, first, to avoid sentiment and emotion. I cannot, to take one example, think of any woman in politics or business who would be comfortable giving the kind of speech Al Gore has given about the car accident that almost killed his son and the lung cancer

that killed his sister. Women simply don't do deathbed dialogue in public. (This is another reason we need more women
in politics.) Nor do many of them want to talk about the thing
their mother told them in the kitchen one day that helped
form their thinking about justice, or the very personal reac-
tion they had once after spending a day with a welfare case-
worker as he made his rounds in Newark. They will tell you
about these things in private conversation, but they usually
won't say them in public.

I think the reason is that they fear that if they speak about
these things they will be labeled and dismissed as . . . women.
As emotional and sentimental and soft. And so they stick to
statistics and assertions. Whereas a lot of men in politics will
speak emotionally at the drop of a hat, because they don't
want to be dismissed as . . . mere men. As cold and uncaring
and hard.

Now, there's more than enough faux emotion in politics in
our time, and I would not advise women, or men, to imitate Al
Gore. (Deeper in this book I will argue against emotionalism
as a rhetorical style.) But if you eschew emotion and high sentiment, ponder whether you do it for good reasons or bad,
with rigidity or honest judgment. Consider whether a particular emotional passage or section of high sentiment is actually
truthful, helpful in making a point and nonmanipulative in
tone and intent. If it is those things it might be used to good
and fair effect.

I think the emotional reticence problem is probably gener-
ational. Women in politics on the national level or high up on
the state level, and women in significant positions in business,
are usually in their forties and fifties and sixties. They grew up
in the Dress for Success era, when women were told to wear
handsome suits and hang out at the water cooler talking to

their male colleagues about football. (Around this time Armani thoughtfully started padding the shoulders of our suits, so we looked like we were wearing football uniforms; we looked like delicate fullbacks as we chatted on about the Giants and the Jets.) This kind of advice, very popular twenty-five years ago, was almost touchingly silly, touching in that it meant well and put such high hopes in such small things, silly because it reduced men to a cliché and persuaded women that progress lay in imitating the cliché.

To eschew emotion and sentiment because one might be taken for a woman is silly. You are a woman. If you are a woman who experiences things through a somewhat emotional prism, so be it, it's not terrible; in many ways the heart is a stronger and more logical organ than the brain. You want to speak in a way that reflects who you are, not in a way that obscures it. Don't operate from fear. To rigidly avoid that which might be taken as "feminine" is not to be liberated but caged.

The second thing women in politics often avoid in a speech is humor. I'm not sure why, but I suspect the reason is linked to the problem of sentiment: A woman is afraid of being dismissed as flighty or insufficiently serious if she makes you laugh.

But the most serious people in the world have used humor to make a point, and always have. (See Lincoln, Abraham; Twain, Mark; etc.)

True wit is a surprise in any person, and always a happy one. Wit from a woman standing on a bare stage and giving you her views is more surprising still. If it is in you, use it.

Wit is a delight. Be delightful when you can.

ADVICE FOR PEOPLE
WHO NEVER WROTE
A SPEECH OR PRETTY MUCH
ANYTHING ELSE

You start with trying to figure out what you want to say. This sounds easy and obvious, but is not always. We're human and tend to have lots of thoughts (often scattered) and more than a few opinions, ideas and insights.

You have to winnow it down. Once you do you're halfway home, for *it is harder to decide what you want to say than it is to figure out how to say it.*

Your speech, as I said, should not as a rule go longer than twenty minutes. This sounds like a limitation but is in fact a liberation. In a ten- or fifteen- or twenty-minute speech you cannot possibly say everything that's on your mind. You have to keep to the essential things.

You should stick to one subject—the trade deficit, the future of the Elks Club, why you support the National Endowment for the Arts. You include and expand on the points that pertain, that explain and support and illustrate your point of view on the subject at hand. Here a kind of intellectual neatness counts; if you try to cram everything in the result won't be comprehensive but jumbled.

This is the essential problem with a typical Bill Clinton speech. Now, Clinton as a speaker is interesting. He is generally considered a good speaker, and in many ways he is. He has a natural warmth and an ease with words that make you want to watch and listen. He has a distinctive voice, a soft growl. When he is campaigning on the stump he often has a kind of casual intensity, which is an interesting thing to see.

Never tongue-tied and never eloquent—six years into his presidency, his only candidates for Bartlett's are "I didn't inhale" and "The era of big government is over"—his easy facility is a two-edged sword. While it suggests a certain command, it also highlights Clinton's prime perceptual problem: that he is too fluid, too smooth, like a real estate salesman talking to a walk-in with a Rolex.

Clinton's biggest problem as a speaker is that he rarely says anything that is intellectually interesting, that is genuinely deep and thoughtful. He has the intensity of a deep and thoughtful person without the depth of a deep and thoughtful person. It's slightly disorienting for his listeners. They walk away saying, "That was good," but if you ask them what he said they don't know. Accolades like this have no shelf life, which Clinton seems to perceive, which is why he's always trying to prove himself—over and over. The depth problem is expressed in Clinton's speeches by a kind of jumpiness. He hops from subject to subject, from this program to that initiative, from soulful exhortations to aggressive assertions. Churchill famously said, of a big showy dessert, "This pudding has no theme." Clinton tends to themeless puddings, strawberries here and bananas there. And his speeches are like this not because he has so much to say, but because he can't decide what to say. So he says everything. But *a speech about everything is a speech about nothing.*

Think of a packhorse. You're an old prospector roaming the hills with a packhorse that carries your tools and provisions. If you pack the horse lightly you can move on and cover a lot of ground, maybe at the end hit gold. But if you put too many sacks on the horse's back it will collapse, you will literally get nowhere, and there's no bonanza at the end.

The fact that you are limited, that you can't pack everything on or in, can liberate you. The fact that you can't say everything, the fact that you have to winnow your thoughts down to the essentials, means that you can get to the heart of the matter quickly. You don't have to add things that are marginal, extraneous; you can stay with what engages you and explore what is important. You don't have time to take false trails, so you don't get lost.

When you are thinking about what you want to say, it is often helpful to define it down, in your own mind, to a sentence or two.

As in, "I want to say the U.S. trade deficit is a really serious problem and we have to pay attention to it."

Or, "I want to say we have to change the way we market our products—we have to find out more about how people make decisions to buy the things we sell."

Or, "I want to say that I'm grateful I was elected PTO president, that I consider it an honor, and that I think it's time we made some changes in how we raise money."

If you can't quite see the sentence in your mind, try to imagine a newspaper headline that reports the content of your speech. "SMITH WARNS COLLEAGUES NOT TO IGNORE RESEARCH AND DEVELOPMENT—'THAT'S WHERE ALL OUR FUTURE PROFITS ARE,' HE SAYS." "WILSON TELLS FOREIGN POLICY GROUP CHINA RE-ARMING 'AT FURIOUS RATE.'" "PINKERTON TELLS KIWANIS: AMERICA WAS RIGHT IN VIETNAM."

Always reduce it down. This keeps it from having a false big-ness in your mind, and allows you to get your hands around it.

Another way to get a handle on what you want to say is to ask: What does this speech have to *do?* Every speech has a job, a reason for being.

Suppose you are asked to appear before a business group whose members have been talking about what appears to be the coming deregulation of the electricity business. You might ask them, "Why me?" Perhaps they answer, "Because we've heard you're a big supporter of deregulation, and we'd like you to make the case for it because whichever way it goes it will have implications for our members." You might ask if the group is skeptical or supportive of deregulation. Let's say the answer is, "Half and half," or—best—"Most of us haven't made up our minds."

So you accept the invitation and sit down and think.

You already know what you want to say: "Deregulation is good." Now you've got your sentence, your headline. The job of your speech is to support the assertion that deregulation is desirable.

You write "Dereg is good" on a yellow legal pad.

Another thought follows: "Good for consumers and good for businesses because it will likely cut electric bills for both by at least 10 percent."

Once you have written this down you will probably follow it with a note to yourself: "Explain what dereg is—allowing independent companies to compete with local utility that now has elec monopoly."

Then: "Cut in rates that will follow dereg could yield maybe $30 billion savings each year—having effect of a major tax cut."

Then: "Competition that dereg will bring will likely yield new products—energy-saving devices. And possible cleaner energy too—breakthroughs in thermal, wind power more likely when companies compete."

Then: "Some people fear, understandably, that new elec companies won't be as reliable as utils. But answer is competition: If company X fails you you'll go to company Y, and if they're good they keep your business and if they're no good you go back to local utility."

And: "State the case of monopolies, they want to go slow, this is understandable from their viewpoint, explain their thinking."

And: "Explain why I think they're wrong. Argue they're thinking more about their own interests than consumers'."

And: "Admit deregulation in general has a bad name— phone companies—makes life more complex, more decisions, and average Joe doesn't think his phone rates went down."

And: "But they did. And phone dereg led to cellulars, beepers, etc., new world of inventions & products. And phones aren't electricity, elec is easier—new company just changes the meter on your house, same elec but new carrier, if you don't like their service you fire them & go back to local utility next day, etc."

And: "Talk about current state of play, political scene, legislation, Calif and New York leading the way, federal government considering."

And: "Talk about which companies are gearing up to compete and what they say they can offer. Paint picture of future if they're right."

* * *

Congratulations. By writing down one sentence you wrote the second and the second brought the third and the third the fourth. You have an outline—the architecture of the speech, the frame of the house. Now all you have to do is furnish it, flesh out each point.

You've only been at work for forty minutes and you think all the hard work is ahead of you, but it's not. The hard work is choosing, organizing, laying the foundation. You've done this. A fifteen-minute speech runs about seven or eight typed double-spaced pages, and you already have three pages of notes.

Most important, you know what you want to say. You know what the speech's job is.

Sometimes the process is harder than others. You're asked to speak and you ask them what they want you to talk about and they answer, with a cheeriness that suggests they think this is good news, "Anything you like!"

Suppose, for instance, it's a speech thanking the state real estate industry for the Salesman of the Year award.

You know you want to say thanks. This is easy because you do appreciate it. And maybe you appreciate it more than most because you've never actually won an award, or at least not since high school when you won Most Likely to Wind up Behind Bars.

But after that, what? What's the speech's job after that? You've got ten minutes to fill.

Well, you might tell them a story. About the people who taught you how to do what you're being honored tonight for doing well.

Or maybe about what almost became your biggest sale ever, and didn't, and what you learned from it.

Or about your first deal, which was touch and go all the way, and what made it work, and who or what helped you.

Or that thing a crusty old agent told you when you were first starting out, and you thought it wasn't true but it was.

You're telling stories. You're giving anecdotes. This is good. Because anecdotes are self-contained, they have a beginning, a middle and an end, and they make your audience see pictures. They'll see the crusty old agent chain-smoking Merits, they'll see the big brick mansion with the broken gate.

Now the audience knows you're a good driver, that you take time to point out interesting things along the way.

Perhaps you want to tell them why you like your job. (This, ahem, only works if it is true.) People who sell houses are helping people find a kind of security, they're sometimes helping them fulfill a dream, or giving a family a new beginning. This may make you remember something. What thinking about it just made me remember is the time a friend of mine bought a beautiful old Bible from a woman who owned a little Bible shop near Rutherford, New Jersey, where my friend and I went to college. He discovered this little shop and found this extraordinary Bible, exquisitely illustrated, and he thanked the woman warmly for selling it to him and added that, frankly, she was charging less than he would expect. She looked him in the eye and said, softly, "I don't sell Bibles, I find good homes for them."

Maybe what gets you going in the morning is a sense that people who sell real estate aren't just selling houses, they're finding good families for them? No? Well, get thinking about this: What do you think of your job as? What service are you performing in society? What's the point of what you do? Do you ever leave a closing and see a couple ride off and have any thoughts about their new life? Are they thoughts that reflect well on your profession, and can be shared?

Or maybe, frankly, lately you don't quite like your job as much as you used to, and maybe there are reasons for your reservations. Maybe they have to do with how your profession is conducted these days, or the effect on the profession of regulations, taxes, the growing potential for lawsuits. Maybe if you express your thoughts—with a certain warmth, and maybe some humor—you will be doing a public good, pointing out some things that could and should be changed by the industry, important members of which are arrayed before you in the audience. (An obvious caution: You can't sound like you're complaining. If you've just been named Salesman of the Year and you're selling and making money, it's not good to sound as if you're not at least relatively happy, as they may stone you.)

Think and write. Put your points and stories in order.

The point is, you've begun. You've got notes. You're concentrating. And you're thinking, perhaps—I hope you are—that you should treat the members of the audience as if they're friends, that you're going to talk to them the way you talk to your friends, with the same candor and trust and respect.

You've been working for an hour. Now you should get up and walk around so your back won't bother you. Have a cup of tea. Call your best friend and tell him what you're doing. He may crack a joke you can use. Keep a pencil by the phone. Anything that makes you laugh will make the audience laugh and can probably be used, with the obvious exception of anything that can be characterized by the old term *off-color*.

After fifteen minutes, come back. Start fleshing out the points you want to make.

Then start typing it all into the computer.

If you find yourself doing draft after draft, this is good. As you write and rewrite you are unconsciously absorbing, picking up your own rhythm and phrasing. This will show itself in a greater ease, a greater engagement when you stand up and give the speech. People will know that you know your text. (Oddly enough, the more tired you get as you write and rewrite, the more likely you are to abandon any self-conscious semi-stentorian writing and write more like yourself. Fatigue lets you emerge. This is good.)

Here we should remember one of the oldest and sturdiest clichés in all of communication. No one knows who said it, it has been attributed to everyone from Aristophanes to Don Hewitt, and it applies not only to speeches but to all kinds of presentations, from documentaries to children's shows to stand-up reports from journalists in front of the White House. It is: *Tell 'em what you're gonna tell 'em—tell 'em—then tell 'em what you told 'em.*

For our purposes this means: Announce your subject and point of view at the beginning of the speech ("It's my belief that the budget deficit is a sleeping giant that will soon come awake and damage our current prosperity"), repeat it in the middle of the speech ("Another reason I think the deficit is dangerous is . . . ") and tie it all up again at the end ("And we must remember that the deficit is a big danger not only to us, but even more to our children").

This may seem simple-minded, but it isn't. It helps refocus your audience, yanks them back to your thoughts if they're starting to daydream. And it keeps you focused, too.

The process you're going through—what do I want to say, what does this speech have to do?—applies to every kind of speech, from "My Travels in the Sudan" at the local Rotary to a major political speech by a major figure.

An example.

When George Bush was to accept the nomination of the Republican party for the presidency in 1988, he knew he had to do two things. I worked with him on the speech, and we often discussed them. The first was obvious. He had to accept the nomination and speak of his gratitude. He knew that he had been chosen from a full field of candidates, that the nomination could have gone to another. He had to say that he was grateful, that he understood the nomination brought with it not only great honor but many responsibilities, the primary one of which, right now, was to reintroduce himself to the American people.

Which was the second thing Bush had to do in the speech. He knew he was famous but unknown, that after eight years as vice president people knew his name but not his thoughts. And so he would have to speak, plainly, about what he believed, about what he thought and why he thought it.

After he thanked the delegates he referred to the "famous but unknown" quandary without, of course, using those words:

> For seven and a half years, I have helped the president conduct the most difficult job on earth. Ronald Reagan asked for, and received, my candor. He never asked for, but did receive, my loyalty. And those of you who saw the president's speech this week, and listened to the simple truth of his words, will understand my loyalty all these years.
>
> But now you must see me for what I am: the Republican candidate for president of the United States. And now I turn to the

American people to share my hopes and intentions, and why and where I wish to lead.

Bush was saying that he was "unknown" because he'd spent the past two administrations doing his job, which was quietly helping the president and being discreet about it.

But now he would speak his mind:

An election that is about ideas and values is also about philosophy. And I have one. At the bright center is the individual. And radiating out from him or her is the family, the essential unit of closeness and of love. For it's the family that communicates to our children—to the twenty-first century—our culture, our religious faith, our traditions and history.

From the individual to the family to the community, and then on out to the town, to the church and the school, and, still echoing out, to the county, the state and the nation—each doing only what it does well, and no more. I believe that power must always be kept close to the individual, close to the hands that raise the family and run the home.

What he was saying here was: I am a conservative, with a conservative's views. But now he advanced it a step, speaking of his personal sense of conservatism:

I am guided by certain traditions. One is that there is a God and he is good, and his love, while free, has a self-imposed cost: We must be good to one another. . . .

And there is another tradition. And that is the idea of community—a beautiful word with a big meaning, though liberal Democrats have an odd view of it. They see community as a limited cluster of interest groups, locked in odd conformity.

In this view, the country waits passive while Washington sets the rules.

But that's not what community means, not to me. For we are a nation of communities, of thousands and tens of thousands of ethnic, religious, social, business, labor union, neighborhood, regional and other organizations, all of them varied, voluntary and unique. This is America: the Knights of Columbus, the Grange, Hadassah, the Disabled American Veterans, the Order of Ahepa, the Business and Professional Women of America, the union hall, the Bible study group, LULAC, Holy Name—a brilliant diversity spread like stars, like a thousand points of light in a broad and peaceful sky.

Does government have a place? Yes. Government is part of the nation of communities—not the whole, just a part.

I don't hate government. A government that remembers that the people are its master is a good and needed thing.

You notice something odd in the "This is America" paragraph. People around Bush, eager as people around candidates always are to include every single group in every single litany, kept shoehorning in groups that were, well, interest groups: the Disabled American Veterans and so on.

Now Bush advanced his explanation of how he thinks and who he is from the abstract "I am a conservative" to the specific: "I am Bush."

Two men this year ask for your support. And you must know us.

As for me, I've held high office and done the work of democracy day by day. Yes, my parents were prosperous, and their children were lucky. But there were lessons we had to learn about life. John Kennedy discovered poverty when he campaigned in West Virginia; there were children there who had no milk. And

young Teddy Roosevelt met the new America when he roamed
the immigrant streets of New York. . . .

Bush here was saying: I know the press is playing me as a
rich preppy, but look what the rich preppies Jack and Teddy
became—great men.

And I learned a few things about life in a place called Texas. . . .

Here he had to break to let the Texas delegation do what
he knew they'd do: go wild.

We moved to West Texas forty years ago, forty years ago this year.
And the war was over and we wanted to get out and make it on
our own. Those were exciting days. We lived in a little "shotgun
house," one room for the three of us. Worked in the oil business, and then started my own.
   And in time we had six children. Moved from the shotgun to
a duplex apartment to a house. Lived the dream—high school
football on Friday nights, little league, neighborhood barbecue.
   People don't see their own experience as symbolic of an era,
but of course we were. And so was everyone else who was taking
a chance and pushing into unknown territory with kids and a
dog and a car. . . .

What Bush was doing was not only telling about his life in a
way that was truthful and specific—he always thought reporters
and profile writers missed the essential point, that though
he'd been born rich he'd hustled hard in Texas to become a
success on his own. But he was also connecting his life to
yours, to everyone who's had a child and lived the life that
children bring with them, sports and school and such. Bush

was also connecting his life to *history*—to the history of those who'd fought World War II and then come home to the cities, and married, and gone on to invent the suburbs of America, the Levittowns and Hempsteads and Midlands. He was telling them: You were part of a saga, though none of us thought of it that way. But you invented modern America.

The speech did what it had to do. Bush went on to fight a good campaign, and won. People still say the acceptance speech elected him, but they are wrong. Bush was going to win that election, and easily, because he was the number-two government official of the eight-year era that brought the biggest peacetime economic expansion in U.S. history and the fall of the Soviet Union. He won because he ran as the man who would continue the policies that yielded those rich fruits. Mike Dukakis, good man that he is, was never going to beat him.

What the acceptance speech did accomplish was to bring Bush a new confidence. The opinion polls had not always been good and the press spoofed him daily. But by gathering his thoughts and asserting them he gave his campaign a theme and his election meaning.

Every speech has a job to do, and no matter who you are, pope, president, poet or pipe layer, if you're giving a speech you have to understand what its job is and work to make sure it's done.

A WORD FROM JAMIE HUMES

Jamie Humes, former speechwriter for seven presidents and gifted impersonator of Winston Churchill, once wrote a good book about speechwriting called *The Sir Winston Method* (Morrow, 1991). In it, Jamie quotes Churchill on those early hours and days when you begin to really think about a speech, to do whatever research might be needed and take notes on what you want to say: "There is in that act of preparing the moment you start caring."

Humes adds, "Only then are you ready to speak to an audience. Because an audience can be *convinced* only when they see you *care* about what you are talking about."

Humes writes that Churchill had a father figure who instructed him on public speaking, an Irish-born American politician named Bourke Cochran, who was considered by Presidents Wilson and Taft to be America's greatest orator. Churchill once asked Cochran the secret of eloquence, and he replied, "Believing in what you are talking about." Cochran summed it up with one word: sincerity.

"It doesn't matter how many statistics or facts you rattle off," writes Humes, "if the audience senses you aren't really committed." He summed up his advice with an old saying that has endured because it is true: "People don't care how much you know unless they know how much you care."

Humes also offers a heartening reminder to those who are procrastinating: "Do you remember back in college or high school when you were assigned a report to write? First it was a chore that you put off doing. But when you finally got down to it, what at first seemed boring became interesting. The more you read, the more you got involved. The more committed you got, the more you cared about what you wrote."

True, yes?

What if you don't care about what you're talking about? Then you are speaking on the wrong subject, and must change it. If you can't, tell those who've assigned the topic that you do not find it engaging and need their help in explaining why it is. This will involve them in your struggle, and may convince them to change your assignment. If they don't, at least they'll be more sympathetic. Ask your colleagues why the topic you have to speak on is interesting—the guest may yield a funny series of anecdotes. And you may actually get interested.

BY THE WAY

O ne of the nice things about writing and giving a speech is that you get to tell your story at your own pace. You are free to make an assertion and back it up with your own points in the order in which they seem important to you.

We don't get this opportunity often enough. In life communication is often more like this: You're having lunch with friends and telling them about, say, a problem your child is having, that she has bad dreams that are beginning to concern you. You say, "Tiffany has been having these nightmares, and they're so scary that when she tells me about them they actually scare *me*. Last night she told me—"

What are the dreams about? an eager friend interrupts.

Um, I want to tell you in just a second, but to understand it there's this thing she said last night that—

Was she up late? That makes children nervous.

Um, um, yes. She couldn't sleep. But she told me that before she falls asleep—

Does she have a Serta? They can be uncomfortable for kids.

Um, I forget. I think I got her a Sealy.

* * *

I think this is what purgatory is going to be like, trying to tell stories to bright and responsive friends who, in their eagerness to get all the details and give you news you can use, wrest control of the narrative from your poor, disorganized self. The questions they ask are pertinent but throw you off your track, making you lose not only some of the facts but sometimes the point of what you're saying. I sometimes think people do this because they're anxious and hope to find relief through controlling the flow of information.

Anyway, in a more polite age this was known as being irritating. Now it is known as being acute: You are the kind of person who can get to the heart of the matter.

My point: When you make a speech you get to do the narrative at your pace and highlight what you think is important. And at the end, you get to take questions.

It can be a real relief, a moment of coherence in a jumbled world.

Some Basics to Note

s you write your speech there are some basics to keep in mind.

You must be able to say the sentences you write. And so they cannot be long and serpentine things that curl around clauses, caress subclauses, encompass extended metaphor, stop briefly for a whimsical digression and culminate, ultimately, in a long and rhythmic peroration that signals to your audience that you would not take it unkindly if they, at just about this moment, would interrupt you with vigorous and sustained applause.

Read that sentence aloud. Difficult, yes? And not just because it's not a great sentence. It's too long to say. You'll run out of breath, emphasize the wrong word, trail off. Also, you'll probably concentrate so hard on saying it right that you'll forget what you're saying.

Keep your sentences sayable, like this. Or like this—and this too—and also this. Churchill thought a speech without dashes was not a speech but a magazine piece. He used the dashes to tell him when to take a breath—when to break the rhythm—what to emphasize. Commas, semicolons and periods do this too, but dashes are easier to see when you're at a podium, easier to understand when you're under the lights.

Once you've finished a first draft of your speech—which, as you know, is a first complete version—stand up and read it aloud. *Where you falter, alter.*

Sentences must be short and sayable not only for you but for your listeners. They're trying to absorb what you say, and if your sentences are too dense with information they won't be able to follow.

First-rate newswriters for network anchormen are prized professionals who do for a living what you're doing: breaking down long and unsayable sentences into shorter, sayable ones. They write for listeners as opposed to readers. (Sometimes when they are tired and the day goes long, TV writers see themselves as convicts on chain gangs with sledgehammers, "breakin' big ones into little ones.")

Reporters for newspapers write for readers. They can write a ten-line sentence for a lead and be completely understood. As in, "In an emotional Oval Office interview this afternoon President William Jefferson Clinton, forty-second president of the United States, announced that he would resign the presidency effective noon tomorrow because of what he called 'the toll on my family and my own emotional well-being of six years of ceaseless, cruel and unfounded attacks on my character, my history and my leadership.' The president's statement, which appeared to be spontaneous and unplanned, was minutes later characterized by a shaken White House aide, who spoke on condition of anonymity, as 'Not something that frankly we were expecting today.'"

But a newswriter for Peter Jennings would break that information down so Peter could say it and we could understand it: "An amazing moment in American history today—Bill Clinton, the president of the United States, has resigned. In an extraordinary meeting with reporters this afternoon the president said he is fed up with what he called six years of 'cruel and unfounded' attacks. The meeting had not apparently been planned, it was called just minutes before it began. When reporters filed in the president spoke to them quickly and briefly. One called it 'Less a statement than an outburst.' Mr. Clinton is with his family right now in the White House residence. He will step down at noon tomorrow. Vice president Albert Gore will become president at that time. He too is at the White House, meeting in his office with aides, including the National Security Advisor. The vice president is scheduled to speak to the nation from the pressroom in just a few minutes. We'll go there as soon as he begins.

"Bill Clinton's bombshell came, as we said, in an Oval Office meeting, at 2:30 this afternoon. Carol Simpson of ABC News was there; she is at the White House now. Carol, you had a front-row seat on history—tell us what happened."

A suggestion: Go out and buy today's *Times, Washington Post* and *Wall Street Journal.* Read the big front-page stories in each. At 6:30 tonight put on the network evening news and listen to how Tom, Peter and Dan tell those stories. Keep what you learn in your head as you write—not their style but their brevity.

It's important as you work to remember that speeches are words in the air. Your audience doesn't have a printed copy to which to refer to clear up any questions. All they have is you, speaking, up there, into a mike.

And so your words must be hearable and comprehensible the first time out. This again may sound obvious and simple but is not always.

A lot of words sound alike. For instance, saver, savor, saber and savior might all sound pretty much alike when spoken from a podium twenty yards away. You may be trying to communicate that the man knew he had a saber, but the audience may be hearing that he knew he had a savior. Often context will make things clear, sometimes not. To find any such potential confusions, read your speech aloud to family or friends and ask them to stop you if they get confused. If they do, stick with the word you want to use if you feel it's the right one, but make it clear by adding a clarifying phrase: "The soldier knew he still had a weapon, a saber strapped to his side. And so he drew it and continued his advance."

Sometimes the comprehension problem involves not a word but a phrase. Once, working on a speech for Vice President Bush, I was trying to capture his thoughts on volunteerism. He wanted to emphasize the personal giving of goods and time as an answer to some of our nation's ills.

I thought about it for a few days and concluded: What he really wants is a kind of muscular altruism. So I put that phrase in his speech. A few days later John Sununu, then a campaign aide and soon to be President Bush's chief of staff, walked up to me, opened the speech that was curled like a Roman senator's in his hand, and pointed.

"Kill muscular altruism," he said.

"Why?"

"Because it sounds like a disease."

I started to laugh. He was exactly right. Bush would be talking about muscular altruism and people would hear muscular dystrophy. Why? Because that's what they're used to—dystrophy is the word after muscular, not altruism. And altruism sounds like a medical condition.

Russell Baker and Richard Cohen would have had a ball: "Bush may think he is right to cut funds for welfare, but volunterism can't solve everything, and he just may find that 'muscular altruism' is for him less a program than a political illness—one that could prove fatal." Harumph, harumph.

A solid Sununu save.

Always think about how things sound, literally the sound that words and phrases make when they leave your mouth and enter a few hundred ears. Think about whether they could be misunderstood. Remember: No one in your audience has a written copy of your speech, all they have is the sound of what you're saying.

The words and phrases you use must not only be "hearable" by the audience, they must be sayable by you.

William Safire, maximum leader of all former White House speechwriters and president for life of the Judson Welliver Society—he was the first presidential speechwriter—compiled some of the great speeches of history in his book *Lend Me Your Ears* (Norton, 1992), which, as Bill would note, is still available at a bookstore near you.

Safire's breezy forward offers good advice for writers and speakers, including this:

"[B]eware of undeliverable words. 'Undeliverable' is one such tripword; it may look easy enough on the page, and it may be easy to pronounce in the mind when read silently, but when the moment comes to push it past your lips, such a word invites a stumble." Safire recalls that as a young speechwriter he drafted remarks for New York City's official greeter, who was to welcome Korea's Syngman Rhee. "I referred to the visiting president's 'indomitable will'; the greeter . . . knew he would say something like 'indomitabubble' and asked for a synonym. When I gave him 'indefatigable' he fired me on the spot; somebody else had to slip him 'steadfast.'" Safire says that in retrospect he now sees he was intransigent.

Here is another problem that can get in the way of comprehension.

Americans used to have accents. They had words and phrases that were particular to those accents, that came with them. Our accents derived essentially from two things, region and ethnicity. You might have had a southern accent, or a Texas accent; if you were from the north you might have had a New York accent or a Boston accent, or a version of the New York or Boston accent that was born within the ghettos of those cities—an Irish accent, or an Italian one.

These accents have not fully disappeared, but they are not as broadly prevalent in our population as they once were. Half a century of mass media, of the steady instruction of TV and radio and movies, has thinned and lessened regional and ethnic ways of speaking. (Rich accents still exist, of course, among our newest immigrants, the Russians, the Filipinos, the islanders of the Caribbean, Pakistanis, Indians and Asians. But their children, born in New York and New Jersey and Ohio and California, will no doubt develop the modern American nonaccent accent.)

A friend of mine argued to me recently that in fact Americans *do* still have accents, but they're no longer defined by region and ethnicity. Now they are connected to age, to generation. People under twenty or twenty-five years of age have the same accent, the "Like, ya know" accent that used to be the sound of Valley Girls and now is the sound of young people across the country. (Because my ten-year-old son and I watch TV too much, he is developing a variation on Likeyaknow, or rather a derivative of it. It is the sitcom accent, based on the way the ten-year-old son of Tim "Tool Time" Taylor talks on *Home Improvement.* Sitcom sounds like this: "Uh, yah, uh, right, mom." This accent even comes with a roll of the eyes.)

As for those over twenty-five or so who are not recent immigrants, most of us are . . . well, the sons and daughters of Cronkite. We speak clearly, with more or less accentless American speech. Perhaps this should be called the Over-twenty-five American Accent, though most of us have retained, thank goodness, some mild regional tics and ethnic tendencies and things we picked up along the way. I still say something I read in a book as a child and absorbed so completely that now it is simply part of how I talk, and how my sisters talk. It is saying "Hey" when you see a friend, instead of "Hi." I do this because when I was twelve I read *To Kill a Mockingbird* and that is how the wonderful young Scout Finch, southern girl, said hello to people: "Hey, Mr. Robbins."

I am about, I swear, to get to my point.

I think that the thing that has replaced accents in America is professional jargon, the shorthand language of shared knowledge. Professions have always had their own jargon of course—"Bogie at three o'clock!" said the airmen in the war movies of my youth—but as technology has intensified and knowledge become more specialized the jargon has gotten thicker.

So thick that it amounts to a kind of dialect.

People in media and politics, workers on Wall Street, doctors and scientists, lawyers and editors, insurance salesmen and journalists and printers and computer programmers: All have, for some time, spoken their own dialects. I vividly remember, when I went to work at CBS News in the 1970s, hearing a young producer bark, "We got a bird at six from Dixie with the lead, Threlkeld wrap, crash and burn." She said this with pride, for she was speaking pure dialect, incomprehensible to any but the initiated, who understood her perfectly: We will receive a satellite transmission at six o'clock that contains a piece by the reporter Richard Threlkeld, who is in Israel; it will be the first story on the evening news tonight and so we will have to work quickly to have it ready for broadcast by 6:30.

So entranced were my young colleagues and I by what we heard in the newsroom each day that we took to barking our own pidgin dialect to the boys on the desk: "A.P. with an Urgent at twelve o'clock high, light-weave polyester." None of us went far at CBS.

But even normal people speak professional dialect now. Even teachers, who were once the most articulate and clear-speaking members of any community, now say, "Do you have an issue?" instead of, "Is something wrong?" and "That is an inappropriate response which I think we may have to moderate," as opposed to "That's bad behavior, stop it."

If you've ever seen the television program *ER*, you've seen a good example of pure dialect. It is clear in that drama that the doctors and nurses and technicians come from different places and classes, but they all have the same adult American nonaccent accent. And when an emergency patient is rolled in on a gurney they rush around in the ER and yell things to each other in pure professional dialect: "GSW, BP 50 over palp, no resp, intubate him stat!"

We increasingly speak in the dialect not of our tribe but of our profession. Because our profession now *is* our tribe.

What does this have to do with public speaking?

Most speakers inevitably lapse into professional dialect when they speak. And this is difficult for audiences. You must keep this in mind, and remember to offer simultaneous translation as you go along. (It's always best to write it into the text.)

As in: "We decided on an IPO, an initial public offering of the stock, in which members of the public would be invited to invest . . . "

Or, "The patient was hemorrhaging from what emergency crews call a GSW—a gunshot wound. His blood pressure was so low we couldn't get a complete read, and he wasn't breathing . . . "

Or, "HR 235, as you know, is the tort reform legislation that a lot of Republicans hope will help cut down on the number of frivolous lawsuits that are now wreaking havoc in the courts."

Why are you saying "as you know"? Because it's polite. Once President Reagan, in a speech that included some relatively arcane information, used "as you know" just before he defined something, and one of his aides scrawled on the margins of the speech, to the speechwriters, "If they know, why are we telling them?"

We answered, "Because a lot of them don't know. But it's rude to show that you, the speaker, assume they, the audience, don't know. So you say 'as you know,' tell them what you figure they may not know, everyone understands and no one is offended. Which, as you know, is important."

By the way, it's not always necessary to provide simultaneous translation: If you're speaking at a professional gathering where everyone can be expected to understand the meaning of the terms you're using, the free use of dialect is good, and a time-saver. But check to see if spouses or others are invited. If they are, they might be a significant part of your audience and may need translation.

LET ME JUST THROW THIS IN

Sometimes you finish a draft of a speech and you're feeling good, the heavy lifting is behind you. That night you set the clock and go to bed, only to be presented, in those brief moments between wakefulness and sleep, with . . . another point. A point you should include because you think it's interesting and might be helpful. But it came too late, the draft is done, you like the flow of it already, you don't know where you'd put the point. You think: Maybe I'm just being a neurotic-perfectionist, anal-compulsive-type person. Then you think: But it is an interesting point.

What's a writer to do? Worry about it tomorrow. Go to sleep.

Okay, it's morning. Do you still remember the point? Then maybe it is worth including.

This happened to me last night. So first thing this morning I wrote the point down:

What's old to you may be new to your audience.

Most people have learned and absorbed so much over the years about their job or profession or area of expertise that they forget to ever mention what used to surprise them. They forget what really interested them early on. But it is these things—the things that once struck you with force and that are now, for you, old news—that are often the most interesting things you could tell people about your field, or people in your field. (Maybe them most of all.)

Perhaps, if you are an airline pilot, you were fiercely dismayed when twenty years ago, during your first week on the job, you flew on trans-Atlantic flights as an observer and saw that the pilots and flight attendants weren't given enough time to rest during stopovers. They always seemed tired, which seemed to you dangerous. You've remembered this for twenty years, and yet haven't mentioned it to anyone in nineteen.

Maybe it was the time you saw a senior partner at your law firm give a brilliant summation in an important case. After he won, you approached him and told him of your admiration for his ability to marshal and condense the facts, especially in such a complicated First Amendment case. And the senior partner shrugged and said, "Garbage in, garbage out." You realized this great and esteemed legal veteran did not see his work through your idealistic eyes. You wondered why, and if he had ever been idealistic, and what might have changed him.

When I think of my first day at CBS News in New York I think of what caught my attention in the big main newsroom: The walls were ringed with clocks telling the time in every major city of the world. It made me feel like I was standing in the center of the universe.

These memories and images can yield something interesting for your audience, either information—even then crew exhaustion seemed a problem—or a picture worth painting.

So don't edit out these memories as you work because they're old news to you. They're new news to someone else. And you didn't forget them because they were meaningful.

* * *

There, that was my small point. I don't know where the editors will put it in the book. I have tagged it onto the chapter called "And So We Begin." We'll see if it stays there. If this book were a speech—and by the way, did I tell you I have tried to write it so it could be spoken?—I'd introduce the point directly: "This is a little off the point, but I want to throw it in on the chance it'll be helpful to someone." People like short digressions, they're a short stop on a long drive.

THE SPEECHES WE KEEP IN OUR HEADS

Your own style can be hard to find, your true sound difficult to locate. It takes time. And it's delicate. You're pursuing self-awareness while fighting off self-consciousness. You have to really look at what you've written, really hear what you say and realize, "Oh, that's how I sound." But you have to keep self-consciousness at bay, because self-consciousness makes you change your style. It often makes you imitate how other people sound. But you don't want to sound like other people. You want to sound like you, only a better, clearer you.

When you are writing a speech you can complicate the process and make things more difficult for yourself by thinking about the famous speeches you keep in your head.

There are many great speeches that we all know, or know parts of. Some are in our memories from school, such as Lincoln's second inaugural. Some are in our heads from media, from the playing and replaying each year of Dr. King's speeches on Martin Luther King Day. Because I admired Bobby Kennedy and had the retentive brain of a seventeen-year-old when he died, I think sometimes of Ted Kennedy's beautiful eulogy—

"Those of us who loved him, and who take him to his rest today . . . "

There are famous speeches from presidents and others, and we know them so well we know the words that precede and follow the famous phrases:

"Ask not what your country can do for you . . . "

"I have a dream . . . "

"Old soldiers never die . . . "

These are all wonderful, and have made their mark on history.

But they each and all came from moments of high state, of great political consequence, and were spoken by famous leaders. And while it is good to be inspired by these speeches, to know them and love them, it is not good to be daunted by them, to think, "This isn't as good as Kennedy's inaugural, I might as well throw in the towel." And it is not good to attempt to imitate them, for you will wind up sounding like the mayor of Springfield on *The Simpsons*: "Let the word go *fawth* in this time and place that the *tawch* has been passed to a new generation of, uh, snow plowers." The mayor of Springfield, in case you're not a *Simpsons* fan, is a buffoon.

Most of us are not great leaders speaking at great moments. Most of us are businessmen rolling out next year's financial goals, or teachers at a state convention making the case for a new curriculum, or nurses at a union meeting explaining the impact of managed care on the hospitals in which we work. And we must have the sound appropriate to us.

Great political speeches tend to have a formality, a certain stentorian sound that is expressed in stately old formulations such as "My fellow citizens . . . " and "our children, and our children's children" and the exhortatory "Let us . . . "

"Let us go forth to lead the land we love," which is what JFK said at the end of his inaugural; "Let us bind the nation's wounds," which every president since Lincoln has said.

"Let us . . . " is a fine old formulation, but like the others it is best left to fine old presidents. Used by nonpresidents and nonleaders it sounds silly.

So hold the lettuce.

Your style should never be taller than you are.

Still, there are things we can learn from the speeches we keep in our heads.

There is often an unadorned quality to sections of great speeches, a directness and simplicity of expression. One reason is that great speeches are composed with concentration, with seriousness: The speaker is so committed to making his point, to being understood and capturing the truth he means to capture, that falseness and furbelows fall away. The result is a striking simplicity and clarity.

While you keep the words of presidents and kings stored in your memory bank, there are some other famous words I want you to put in, if they're not there already, because we can learn something from them.

Stop here and go out and rent *The Godfather, Part II*. In the middle of that movie, you will find a speech that is one of the most famous of our time, and that a lot of people keep parts of in their heads. (If I were making a compendium of great speeches of the latter half of the twentieth century I would include it.)

It is the speech spoken by the actor Lee Strasberg, who played the part of Hyman Roth, a character inspired by the old gangster Meyer Lansky.

Strasberg was for many years the leader of the Actors Studio, which famously promulgated certain theories of acting that came to be derided by some classicists and Shakespeareans. Whatever your views on the Method, I think Strasberg's work in this film singlehandedly redeemed the Studio from years of . . . well, Ben Gazzara's kitchen sink macho and Kim Stanley's *tremulo lippolo* in movies like *The Actress.*

I'm digressing. But it's not so bad to get people seeing pictures of Ben Gazzara in an undershirt and Kim Stanley in a car.

Here is Lee Strasberg's great speech, given as Hyman Roth stood, weak and furious, before cold-eyed Michael Corleone:

> There was this kid I grew up with. He was younger than me, sort of looked up to me, you know. We did our first work together, worked our way out of the street. Things were good, we made the most of it. In Prohibition we ran molasses into Canada, made a fortune—your father too.
>
> As much as anyone I loved him and trusted him.
>
> Later on he had an idea: to build a city out of a desert stopover for GIs on the way to the coast.
>
> That kid's name was Moe Green. And the city he invented was Las Vegas.
>
> This was a great man, a man of vision and guts. And there isn't even a plaque or a signpost or a statue of him in that town.
>
> Someone put a bullet through his eye. No one knows who gave the order. When I heard it, I wasn't angry. I knew Moe, I knew he was headstrong, talking loud, saying stupid things. So when he turned up dead, I let it go.
>
> And I said to myself, This is the business we've chosen. I didn't ask who gave the order. Because it had nothing to do with business.

You have two million in a bag in your room. I'm going in to
take a nap. When I wake, if the money's on the table I'll know I
have a partner. If it isn't I'll know I don't.

*That man's name was Moe Green. And the city he invented was
Las Vegas.*

When Mario Puzo and Francis Ford Coppola wrote those
words they thought they were writing dialogue, a theatrical
speech for a major character. But . . . they were writing a great
speech.

It is simple, unadorned, direct, declarative. There isn't anything in it that is "eloquent," and yet taken as a whole it is
deeply eloquent: It tells you something big in an unforgettable
way. There is in it no obvious, signaled rhythm, and yet if you
read it aloud you will find in it the beautiful, unconscious
rhythm of concentrated human speech. There are no phrases
that seem to attempt to conjure up pictures, and yet when you
hear it you imagine a Moe Green and see the dusty nothing-
ness of early Las Vegas.

It is simplicity that gives the speech its power. Each word
means something and each seems to inevitably follow the
word that precedes it and summon the word that follows. And
so a kind of propulsion is created: It moves forward, and with
good speed.

One of the great things about this speech is that as you
hear it you realize that for the first time you're hearing what
Hyman Roth really thinks. The plain and unadorned quality
of his words signals this. And we pick the signal up because *we
have gained a sense in our lives that true things are usually said
straight and plain and direct.*

Most of the important things you will ever say or hear in
your life are composed of simple, good, sturdy words. "I love

you." "It's over." "It's a boy." "We're going to win." "He's dead."

These are the words of big events. Because they are big you speak with utter and unconscious concentration as you communicate them. You unconsciously edit out the extraneous, the unneeded. (When soldiers take a bullet they don't say, "I have been shot," they say, "I'm hit.")

Good hard simple words with good hard clear meanings are good things to use when you speak. They are like pickets in a fence, slim and unimpressive on their own but sturdy and effective when strung together.

(The only bad thing about the Hyman Roth speech is that young Hollywood producers often quote it, changing "This is the business . . . " to "This is the life we have chosen." It is their way of ironically noting that Hollywood is a tough place. But in this they seem to me like the young men and women of Wall Street and Capitol Hill who use the language of war— holding positions, closing fronts, calling in air cover, making strategic retreats—to talk about business deals and legislation. When I hear them I sometimes wince because they remind me of how I spoke when I was twenty-five, for I too appropriated the metaphors of others. What had I done to earn the right to the metaphors? Not much. That's why I used them. Pascal said doctors wear tall hats because they can't cure you. Kids starting out talk like veterans because they're not. The reason I'm on this small rant is this: When you adopt the language of others it usually doesn't make you seem more like them but less. It highlights the differences. It's like wearing a sign that says, "I'm talking big because I'm small." So don't do it. Because you're not small. You're just young. Be patient, the metaphors of your life will come, and you will earn them.)

* * *

Another thought on the words you choose when you write. It is not good to flee a longer, more demanding or more unusual word when you write if it is the right word, the one you first thought of naturally as you formulated your thought. If you feel it is the right word, use it. You don't have to dumb it down. But never strain for a long or demanding word if it does not present itself naturally. If a plain word presents itself first, take that.

An example of the power of plain words:

In late 1996 the writer Tom Wolfe made a speech in New York in which, according to a Talk of the Town piece in the *New Yorker*, he raised doubts about the spirit and assumptions of modern science. He quoted Nietzsche and questioned whether science would not ultimately destroy its own foundations. As Wolfe summed up his argument, reporter Jay Fieden wrote, "Wolfe's voice dropped to a stage whisper; 'Suddenly I had a picture in my mind of the whole fantastic modern edifice collapsing and man suddenly dropping—stricken!—into the primordial ooze. And he's there floundering around, and he's treading ooze and wondering what's going to become of himself. And suddenly something huge and smooth swims underneath him and boosts him up. He can't see it! He doesn't know what it is! But he's very much impressed. And he gives it a name: God.'"

This is the right stuff. You would never, in an audience, not listen to this, not hear it. Its driving-forward rhythm communicates the speaker's excitement. You can also see it in the swiftness of his imagery—edifice collapsing, man dropping, force lifting. But for me the power of Wolfe's style is seen in two simple words: huge and smooth.

A less gifted writer, knowing he was about to introduce God, would have employed big, godlike words—incredibly vast, colossal. But *huge* and *smooth* made me think as I read (and would have made me think as I heard) of a submarine, and then of a big hand—God's big hand. Which I saw once he got to the word God.

Only a confident communicator, *one who knows he can use the word he's thinking,* the word that came naturally to him, can talk like that.

Let me make a last point about words and the power of simplicity. (I am asking you to let me out of respect, and also letting you know that if I'm being boring it will be over soon.)

When I was a teenager I used words like "coruscatingly" and "obfuscate" and "ameliorate." They are good words and I still use them, but not as much. The reason is connected to what I said about young Hollywood producers and the Hyman Roth speech.

It's that when you are young and life is less packed with events, history, knowledge and experience, your vocabulary is often more elaborate, as if to make up for the lack. You want to show that you're alive to the bigness of adulthood and its thoughts.

As you grow older and life itself becomes more elaborate and complex, you find yourself using simpler words. And this is not only because your brain cells are dying. It is also, for some of us, because you have grown used to life, even comfortable with it, and understand that it comes down to essentials, that the big things count and the rest is commentary, and that way down deep in the heart of life's extraordinary complexity is . . . extraordinary simplicity.

I think that to achieve true adulthood is to understand the simplicity of things. We're locked in a funny arc, most of us, in terms of what we know. When you are goony and fourteen

years old you think the most important thing in life is love.
Then you mature, become more sober and thoughtful, and
realize the most important thing in life is achieving, leaving
your mark—making breakthroughs in the field of science, or
winning an Academy Award in recognition of a serious body of
work, or creating security for yourself and your family through
having a good house and sending your kids to good schools.
And then you get old and realize . . . the most important thing
in life is love. Giving love to others and receiving it from God.
All the rest, the sober thoughtful things, are good and constructive . . . but love is the thing. The rest is just more or less
what you were doing between fourteen and wisdom.

The language of love is simple, it is simplicity itself. The
great novelist Edith Wharton noted this when she talked
about romantic love. She said that no matter what the gift of
the writer, whether genius or dunce, the language of love letters is always the same: "I love you, I love you, my darling, you
are so wonderful . . . "

The language of love is simple because love is big. *And big
things are best said, are almost always said, in small words.*

All right, let's cool off and get back to politics.

Here is another speech to keep in mind as you write, for it
too is marked by lovely simplicity.

The best speech at the Democratic National Convention in
1996 was not Bill Clinton's or Al Gore's but that of the actor
Christopher Reeve. Reeve's speech promised to be memorable,
if only for the moving sight of a paralyzed man in a wheelchair
gallantly addressing a throng from a stage. But it was a truly
impressive speech because in it he said things that he believed
to be true, and said them in a strikingly simple way.

Listen:

Over the last few years we've heard a lot about something called family values. And like many of you I've struggled to figure out what that means. But since my accident I've found a definition that seems to make sense. I think it means that we're all family, and that we all have values. And if that's true, if America really is a family, then we have to recognize that many of our family are hurting.

He was talking about how he was *thinking* about a great question, who we are and what we owe each other. And though "hurting" in this context is one of those horrid boomer clichés, Reeves could get away with it.

... One of the smartest things we can do about disability is invest in research that will protect us from disease and lead to cures. This country already has a long history of doing that.

He is asking for money but doing it graciously: We need more, but then giving is an American tradition.

During my rehabilitation I met a young man named Gregory Patterson. When he was innocently driving through Newark, New Jersey, a stray bullet from a gang shooting went through his car window right into his neck, and severed his spinal cord. Five years ago he might have died. Today because of research he's alive. But merely alive is not enough. We have a moral and an economic responsibility to ease his suffering and prevent others from experiencing such pain. And to do that, we don't need to raise taxes. We just need to raise our expectations.

He is painting a picture; you're seeing it as he's saying it. He makes a point to call Patterson innocent because he wants you to know this wasn't some lowlife gangbanger but a person like you, and that it could happen to you.

At the end of this section he will say, and will say again, "This is not a partisan exhortation." Now, the canny Reeve is a very partisan fellow, the former head of the left-liberal Creative Coalition, but he knows that sometimes the best way to be effectively partisan is to be rhetorically nonpartisan.

. . . On the wall of my room when I was in rehab was a picture of the space shuttle blasting off, autographed by every astronaut now at NASA. On top of the picture it says, "We found nothing is impossible." That should be our motto. Not a Democratic motto, not a Republican motto, but an American motto. Because this is not something one party can do alone. It's something we as a nation must do together.

So many of our dreams at first seem impossible. Then they seem improbable. And then, when we summon the will, they soon become inevitable. . . .

This was rousing.

The whole speech was rousing. Part of the reason: his language was so simple and plain, his sentences were like sentences in conversation, short and to the point. Because of the nature of his injury, Reeve cannot breathe without assistance. He has to pause and take in air from a tube; as he speaks he exhales. And so his sentences and phrases had to be short and sharp, no words could be wasted, he didn't have time for show-off stuff. Each word had its own weight and dropped like a smooth coin.

Keep this in mind as you write.

By the way, on "painting pictures": I think it is natural to humans but particularly natural today, in a media-saturated environment, for people to be doing two or three things while they're listening. I watch TV and read newspapers at the same time. My son monitors *The X-Files* and draws illustrations for the fourth-grade sports newspapers at the same time. This may not be good, but I suspect it's true of a lot of us. So when you stand and speak it is good, if you can, and if it is appropriate to what you're saying, to give people the outlines of a picture that they can fill in with their imaginations as you speak. Like the fellow who was driving through Newark and was shot in the neck.

If you don't, they will probably come up with their own pictures and imaginings, which may not have anything to do with what you're trying to say.

SIMPLICITY, II

I had another thought after I finished the last chapter. Fifty years ago there was a play on Broadway, a drama about a teacher who was sent into a small Welsh coal mining town to teach the children there. There amidst the slag heaps she found a quiet young miner whom she began to tutor. He wrote for her an essay about his work. He said it was hard and grim but there were compensations, even moments of transcendence. He described the fierce joy that sometimes seized him when he was down deep in the earth where the corn is green.

When she read those four words—"the corn is green"—she realized the young man was gifted, a writer. (A less gifted one would have written, "where you can see that certain forms of vegetation are beginning to grow.") And so the teacher began her struggle to wrest the boy from the mines and get him into university, where his gifts might blossom.

Simplicity gives you things you can see.

And sometimes hear.

I said before that it's not always a good idea to look to the work of the great for assistance, but Lincoln can help us here, so let's look at two speeches.

Now, when I think of Abraham Lincoln as orator I sometimes think, and forgive me, of the scene in *Close Encounters* when the spaceship has landed and disgorged its content of airmen who had disappeared in World War II. None of them had aged. A scientist who is watching says, wonderingly, "Einstein was right." The man he spoke to answers, as he looks at the little genius extraterrestrials who are now walking out of the spaceship, "Einstein was probably one of them."

I think Lincoln was a kind of genius angel, that there was an otherworldly quality to his life, his leadership, and his writings. His speeches were great for many reasons and in many ways, but one of the elements of his greatness was simplicity of expression. Not always, of course—"We cannot dedicate, we cannot consecrate, we cannot hallow this ground" is not, in a strict sense, simple.

But this is. Here in his second inaugural Lincoln sums up the cause of four years of hard history in one sentence:

> Both parties deprecated war, but one of them would *make* war rather than let the nation survive, and the other would *accept* war rather than let it perish, and the war came.

And the war came. Four clean and simple words that say everything, and in a way that is so unassuming, so flat and compressed that you can hear the cannon roar.

You have to have confidence to write like that. But you don't have to have any particular confidence in your own mastery to *talk* like that. Because that is pretty close to how intelligent people talk when they're *thinking*.

Lincoln's second inaugural contains a beautiful and justly famous phrase: "With malice toward none, with charity for all, with firmness in the right as God gives us to see the right." It follows a less famous but quite powerful section:

> Neither party expected for the war the magnitude or the duration which it has already attained. Neither anticipated that the *cause* of the conflict might cease with or even before the conflict itself should cease. Each looked for an easier triumph, and a result less fundamental and astounding. Both read the same Bible and pray to the same God, and each invokes His aid against the other. It may seem strange that any men should dare to ask a just God's assistance in wringing their bread from the sweat of other men's faces, but let us judge not, that we not be judged. The prayers of both could not be answered. That of neither has been answered fully. The Almighty has His own purposes.

This is breathtakingly succinct; it fully captures the reality of both sides; and with what deft shrewdness it reminds Lincoln's listeners of the moral dimension of the war. He quotes "judge not," but his language—"from the sweat of other men's faces"—judges, slyly but surely.

I'm going to quote another Lincoln speech, this one not so well known, because again there are a few words at the end that pack a wallop. In 1858, two years before his election to the presidency, citizen Lincoln gave a Fourth of July address. He noted that America has among her citizens those descended by blood from the signers of the Declaration of Independence, and those who are not, who are newer arrivals. Of them he said, "when they look through that old Declaration they find, 'We hold these truths to be self-evident, that all men are created equal,' and then they feel that that moral sentiment evidences their relation to those men, and that they have a right to claim it as though they were blood of the blood, and flesh of the flesh, of the men who wrote that Declaration, and so they are."

And so they are. That's one big moving assertion in four short words. Senator Slade Gorton of the state of Washington quoted this speech in one of his own on July 4, 1994, at an oath-taking ceremony for thousands of Asians and Europeans and Africans and Latin Americans who that day became citizens of the United States. Gorton followed Lincoln's quote with, "Welcome to a heritage in which you are equal to all other Americans, no matter how long they or their ancestors have been here.

"Welcome to your citizenship.

"Welcome to America."

That was a nice way to show new Americans that they've joined an old idea and, by joining, made it young again.

THE MOST MOVING THING IN A SPEECH IS ALWAYS THE LOGIC

P oliticians often tell their speechwriters, "I want to be really moving, I want a lot of music and poetry." CEO's do it too: They tell their writers, "Make my speech emotional, with a lot of schmaltz."

Even normal people now think a good speech has to make people cry. And they think the way to do it is to use a lot of rhetorical flourishes and sentimental stories. I remember a few years ago a very smart woman who is a conservative activist was addressing a conservative group about the future of the movement. She said a lot of sensible things about Congress, and pending legislation, and then at the end she veered off into a long and unfortunately not directly relevant anecdote about the death of Dwight Eisenhower. It wasn't indirectly relevant either. It was a stretch, and you could see that she made it because she wanted to make the audience cry. But nothing dries up the tear ducts like a speech that commands you to blubber.

She quoted Eisenhower on his deathbed, and told of how he'd given an old friend a goodbye salute, and as she said it she saluted too. Silence. Then mild applause. They didn't

respond as if they'd been moved, they responded as if someone had tried to manipulate them. Naturally they resisted.

Up till then she'd given a good speech. But the speech had
been so important to her she had overthought it, abandoned
her natural common sense and bowed to the cliché that
you've got to close with a clincher, got to have a boffo ending.
When—and I want you to listen to me on this—you don't.
You don't have to have a boffo ending. And you should never try
to make them cry. You should try to make them, or help them,
think. If you focus on that you may wind up being so clear, so
persuasive, so strong in the good and decent argument that
you're making that . . . they may weep.

Also, clinchers can be a problem because people tend to
deliver them as if they're . . . clinchers. The speaker begins to
act, and acting undercuts the message. Recently a nice and
intelligent man came to my home to sell me an insurance policy. As part of the process he brought out a lot of graphs and
boards with data on them, and in trying to convince me that
long-term financial planning is necessary, and that he happens to provide such services, he dramatically looked me in
the eye and said, "So many people who make a good salary
wind up at the end with nothing. They didn't plan to fail—
they failed to plan." I looked him in the eye right back and
could not suppress a smile, which became a giggle.

He started to laugh too, and rolled his eyes.

"Do you always say that sentence in the middle?" I asked.
"No," he said, "I usually use it at the end, but sometimes I forget." He told me it is a famous line, and that another salesman
in his firm recently sat down with a couple trying to sell them
and just at the moment he got to the line his chair began to
break. As he grabbed the table to keep from falling he blurted,
"They didn't flail to pan—they panned to flail!" He didn't

make the sale. But my salesman did, for he had dropped his
pose, stopped acting and become a person.

It's fine to be moving if you can be and should be, if you're
sincere and truly feel that your subject is one that truly lends
itself to high sentiment. But before you wage a long twilight
struggle to touch the face of God on the city on a hill, keep
this in mind:

The most moving thing in a speech is always the logic. It's never
flowery words and flourishes, it's not sentimental exhortations, it's never the faux poetry we're all subjected to these
days. It's the logic, the thinking behind your case. A good case
well argued and well said is inherently moving. It shows
respect for the brains of the listeners. There is an implicit
compliment in it. It shows that you're a serious person and
understand that you are talking to other serious persons.

The big misconception that speeches should make people cry
is not entirely new. It's only more prevalent, more accepted as
the common wisdom. When the famed orator Edward Everett
spoke before Lincoln at Gettysburg, he went on for more than
two hours and pulled out all the stops with poetry and plead-
ing and stentorian phrases. Then Lincoln got up and offered
a masterpiece of compression, two or three minutes on the
meaning of the war and the meaning of the day. It sounded
dry; he offered no stories of battlefield heroism, made no
great promises of victory, did not stoop to rouse. Instead he
defined the meaning of the war, put it into historical context,
and gave the country insight into the commander in chief's
understanding of the astounding drama of the past three
years. He said that eighty-seven years ago a new nation was
born, that it was founded on the extraordinary idea that all
men are created equal, and that we are now in a war that will

decide whether such a nation founded in such a way will be able to continue and live. Today we honor those who died to ensure that it will. But nothing we say can honor them as much as their actions have honored them. Our true duty now is to take strength from their sacrifice, win the war, preserve our country and expand its founding idea.

It was a speech about the thinking of the president. It contained the logic of the war. In time people understood how beautiful it was, and were moved by it, and learned it by heart; it became a great document of the Republic. But again, it became these things because it was a thoughtful speech, a speech that defined things. *Its logic was moving.*

Everett understood. He listened, knew what had been said, and to the extent that he and Lincoln had been engaged in a rhetorical duel, he knew who won. With great grace he wrote Lincoln, "I shall be glad if I could flatter myself that I came as near to the central idea of the occasion in two hours as you did in two minutes." Lincoln replied with equal grace: "In our respective parts yesterday, you could not have been excused to make a short address, nor I a long one. . . ."

Why the recent emphasis on the idea that a good speech must be flowery and sentimental and make people cry?

Reagan. He was so often moving and so often successful in his speeches that he came to set the standard. But Reagan as a speaker has been misunderstood. He *was* often moving, but *he was moving not because of the way he said things, he was moving because of what he said.* He didn't say things in a big way, he said big things.

The writers and reporters and historians listening to Reagan's speeches didn't always understand this. He could rise in the Palace of Westminster in London in 1982 (!), for example, declare the sure coming demise of the Soviet Union and explain the reasons for it, but many of the writers and reporters and historians who were listening did not understand that they were hearing something striking, thoughtful, historically acute. They thought what they were hearing was Cold War tub-thumping. (Some of them were ideologically wedded to the idea of progress through negotiation; an implicit statement that negotiation is not an end in itself and in this case probably wouldn't solve the problem seemed to them not a reasoned view but a faux pas.)

Writers, reporters and historians were in a quandary in the Reagan years. "The people," as they put it, were obviously impressed by much of what Reagan said; this could not be completely dismissed. But Reagan, they felt, rarely said anything intelligent and thoughtful. And so they decided, and declared, that the people were moved by Reagan because of the wonderful way he said things. He was the Great Communicator.

Which he was. But it wasn't because of how he said things. It was because of what he said.

Let's look at the speech in Westminster for a moment. It began with an overview:

> We're approaching the end of a bloody century plagued by a terrible political invention: totalitarianism. Optimism comes less easily today, not because democracy is less vigorous but because democracy's enemies have refined their instruments of repression. Yet optimism is in order because day by day democracy is proving itself to be a not at all fragile flower. From Stettin on the Baltic to Varna on the Black Sea, the regimes planted by totalitarianism have had more than thirty years to establish their legitimacy. But none—not one regime—has yet

been able to risk free elections. Regimes planted by bayonets do not take root.

He lauds Solidarity, damns the Soviet invasion of Afghanistan, warns that "self-delusion in the face of unpleasant facts is folly." There is an arms race in which "the West must, for its own protection, be an unwilling participant." The forces of totalitarianism, he says, continue to "seek subversion and conflict around the globe."

What then must we do?

We must recognize as Churchill did that the Soviets do not so much want war as the fruits of war and the expansion of their power. In response, as Churchill advised, we must commit ourselves to preserving both freedom and peace.

How? We must start with an understanding of our position. Our adversary is not strong but weak—and getting weaker:

I believe we live now at a turning point. . . . In an ironic sense, Karl Marx was right. We are witnessing today a great revolutionary crisis, a crisis where the demands of the economic order are conflicting directly with those of the political order. But the crisis is not happening in the free, non-Marxist West, [it is happening in] the home of Marxism-Leninism, the Soviet Union. It is the Soviet Union that runs against the tide of history by denying human freedom and human dignity to its citizens.

He lays out the facts of the failure: a Soviet economy in decline, with growth half of what it was in the 1950s. With an entire fifth of its population in agriculture, it still cannot feed its people. The economy is overcentralized, offers no incentives, pours its resources into arms production. The result for the people of the Soviet Union is widespread suffering. The result in the West must be new resolve:

> The hard evidence of totalitarian rule has caused in mankind an uprising of the intellect and will. Whether it is the growth of the new schools of economics in America or England, or the appearance of the so-called new philosophers in France, there is one unifying thread . . . rejection of the arbitrary power of the state, the refusal to subordinate the rights of the individual to the superstate, the realization that collectivism stifles all the best human impulses.

He argues that this new spirit will spread.

> We cannot ignore the fact that even without our encouragement there [have] been and will continue to be repeated explosions against repression. . . . The Soviet Union itself is not immune to this reality. Any system is inherently unstable that has no peaceful means to legitimize its leaders. In such cases, the very repressiveness of the state ultimately drives people to resist it, if necessary, by force.

What to do after realizing that the Soviet Union is in decline? We must declare our objectives firmly, move toward them quickly, recognize that freedom isn't "the sole prerogative of the lucky few" but "the right of all human beings." We must encourage and assist democracy and its essential parts—a free press, free speech, religious freedom—around the globe. We must resist the Soviet Union's covert assistance to Communist rebels in other countries, and help those countries develop democratic institutions.

This is a plan, he says, that will "leave Marxism-Leninism on the ash heap of history."

He says the U.S. will continue to try to move forward on arms talks that will reduce weapons on both sides. He declares again that our military strength is a prerequisite to peace, but adds that it is maintained in the hope it will never be used. He ends with the declaration that hope now is realistic, that "a new age is not only possible but probable," that what Churchill said in 1945 is true for us today:

> When we look back on all the perils through which we have passed and at the mighty foes that we have laid low, and all the dark and deadly designs that we have frustrated, why should we fear for our future? We have come safely through the worst.

And so, said Reagan in summation, have we.

The heart of this speech was a logical argument about what the president saw as the great challenge of our time, and an explanation of what he was convinced we must do to meet it. You can agree or disagree with him on the nature of the challenge or the usefulness of his recommendations, but you cannot read (or hear) this speech without realizing that it is well thought out, that his views are clearly explained, his recommendations strongly asserted.

Was it a moving speech? Yes, very. But moving because it was serious and logical, not sentimental or flowery or poetic. (It was about as poetic as a broom.)

There was a lot to chew on in it, and it was high fiber, no empty calories. (It was sly, too: The ash heap of history, of course, is where Trotsky said the West would wind up.)

The moral, ladies and gentlemen?

It's alright if you want to include in your speech a touching story or a lovely phrase. And as you write these things may emerge. But they are not essential. Keep your attention on the essentials—your argument, your point of view, the truth you are trying to convey.

Your speech doesn't need music, it needs logic. And the good news is logic can be very moving indeed.

I guess I could have boiled all this down—and it's good discipline to try to reduce things to their essence—to this:

Many speakers these days, particularly politicians, want to and think they need to "speak from the heart." And they have reason to want to sound this way. People on TV will compliment them if they do. Anchors and reporters will say, with an approving nod, "As he opened the new memorial to FDR, President Clinton spoke from the heart." And, "Former President Bush clearly connected with his listeners today as he spoke from the heart about why he jumped from that plane."

Everyone likes to be complimented. Everyone wants approval.

But there was once a time, long ago, when politicians didn't seem to think they had to sound as if they were speaking emotionally or personally. They thought they had to speak intelligently, and persuasively. And I believe we can learn something from the forms of yesterday.

The only organ to which no appeal is made these days—you might call it America's only understimulated organ—is the brain. It would be a great relief, and might even be a kind of breakthrough, if an important politician would take an approach something like this:

> My friends, we are not composed only of feelings, we do not consist solely of sentiments. We have hearts, but we have minds too. And so tonight I'm going to speak to you straight from the brain.

I appeal to your brains, my fellow countrymen, and I hope they
hear me as we consider the crucial and difficult issue of . . .

Well, something like that.
But it would be nice to see our minds get some attention.

May I indulge in another Reagan moment? This is a story
about how widespread the idea really is that speeches can be
successful without saying anything serious. It's so widespread
that even highly sophisticated and intelligent people believe it.

One summer evening in 1996 I was at a dinner at an ante-
bellum mansion on the bay of Charleston. The gentleman
who was our host had invited friends from New York, Washington and points south, and among them was a man who was
considering running for the presidency. By luck I was seated
with him at a table full of bright and voluble people who were
full of opinions on the political scene. The talk turned to President Reagan, and the gentleman considering running for
president—I will call him the Politician—talked sweetly about
the experience of hearing Reagan speak. He spoke of Reagan's rhetoric, and said with what appeared to be approbation
that the most interesting thing about Reagan's speeches was
that the best of them were about nothing.

Everyone nodded but I was perplexed, and asked him what
he meant.

He said, "Well, take the Pointe du Hoc speech, for instance.
It was beautiful and touching, but it wasn't really 'about' anything."

I was astonished by this assertion, and told the Politician it
was probably the only stupid one he had ever made in his life.

He laughed, but now he was surprised. "Tell me why I'm
wrong," he said.

And so I did, beginning with some history, which I remembered well for I had worked on the speech.

The Pointe du Hoc speech, which President Reagan gave in Normandy in June of 1984, on the fortieth anniversary of D-Day, is famous for its tribute to the American Rangers who had landed on the beach below that great day, who had braved the Nazi guns, climbed the cliffs, and taken back the continent of Europe.

The old soldiers now sat before him. And Reagan, after speaking of the heroism of all the allied troops, spoke specifically to and of the Rangers: "These are the boys of Pointe du Hoc. These are the men who took the cliffs."

Reagan was moved, the men were moved; you had to be a stone not to be moved. And that of course is what people remember when they remember the speech.

But the Rangers, the invasion, D-Day—that was the *text* of the speech, its obvious subject. The *subtext*—the subtle thing that is really being addressed—was foreign policy right now, in Europe, in 1984.

The Pointe du Hoc speech was about the western alliance. It was about NATO. It was about the Soviet Union.

In 1984 the western alliance was going through great strain. Reagan's election in 1980 had taken Europe aback: Who was this nuclear cowboy? In the first few years following his election U.S.–Soviet arms talks stalled; the Soviets had deployed SS-20 missiles, which they aimed at the great cities of Europe, and Reagan had put forth a two-tiered response: a proposal to eliminate all intermediate range nuclear weapons by both sides in Europe coupled with an announcement that if the Soviets would not agree to this, America would deploy Pershing II and cruise missiles in Europe as a counter to the SS-20s.

The Reagan proposals were controversial, to say the least. A new peace movement swept across Europe, the nuclear freeze movement began in America, and Reagan was blamed for war-mongering. Mitterand of France and Trudeau of Canada refused to back the U.S. approach. The Soviets walked out of ongoing arms talks. To add to the misery, western Europe refused to back U.S. sanctions against the Soviets after the Soviet crackdown on Poland.

Things were not good in the alliance; things in fact were more strained than ever. And so Reagan used the Pointe du Hoc speech to remind the NATO countries of what we had achieved that day forty years ago when we had stuck together: We had defeated tyranny, arm in arm. That is why Reagan evoked the Allied heroism of Normandy Beach—to reinspire the West, and the leaders of the West. That is why he spoke of the courage of Lord Lovat of Scotland, who with his men took Sword Beach and advanced under fire playing bagpipes. That is why he lauded the courage of the French Resistance, and the impossible valor of the Polish cavalry, and the daring of the Canadians who stormed ashore at Juno Beach. He was evoking old heroes to tell their children: Hold together now, have courage, keep heart, we liberated Europe once and if we stay together we will not only keep her free but who knows . . . we may even liberate the Soviets themselves.

And that, I said, is what the speech is "about."

The Politician listened, nodded and, polite man that he is, said he would reread the speech and reconsider his assertion.

The next day I went through my files and found the speech. After speaking of the events of D-Day, Reagan spoke of the rebuilding of Europe, the Marshall Plan, and the coming together of old foes.

Then:

Not all that followed the end of the war was happy or planned. Some liberated countries were lost. The great sadness of this loss echoes down to our own time in the streets of Warsaw, Prague, and East Berlin. The Soviet troops that came to the center of this continent did not leave when peace came. They are still there, uninvited, unwanted, unyielding. The only territories we hold are memorials like this one, and the graveyards where our heroes rest.

We in America have learned bitter lessons from two world wars: It is better to be here, ready to protect the peace, than to take blind shelter across the sea, rushing to respond only after freedom is lost. We have learned that isolationism never was and never will be an acceptable response to tyrannical governments with expansionist intent.

But we try always to be prepared for peace; prepared to deter aggression; prepared to negotiate the reduction of arms; and, yes, prepared to reach out again in the spirit of reconciliation.

In truth, there is no reconciliation we would welcome more than a reconciliation with the Soviet Union, so that together we can lessen the risks of war, now and forever. . . .

(W)e in the United States do not want war. We want to wipe from the face of the Earth the terrible weapons man now has in his hands. I tell you we are ready to seize that beachhead—but there must be some sign from the Soviet Union that they are willing to move forward, that they share our desire and love for peace, that they will give up the ways of conquest. There must be a changing there. . . .

We will pray forever that some day that changing will come. But for now, particularly today, it is good and fitting to renew our commitment to each other, to our freedom, and to the alliance that protects it.

We are bound today by what bound us forty years ago, the

same loyalties, traditions and beliefs. And we are bound by reality: The strength of America's allies is vital to the United States, and the American security guarantee is essential to the continued freedom of Europe's democracies. We were with you then; we are with you now.

Well, "the changing" came; and now a great international question is whether to allow Russia, our new ally, into NATO.

Anyway, the Pointe du Hoc speech wasn't about sentiment, it was about policy. And without that girding of policy none of the facade of sentiment would have stood.

A moment for a small lecture.

The Politician thought the speech at Pointe du Hoc was about nothing in part, no doubt, because he is sophisticated.

Sophisticated people tend to think that speeches are magic. They are like the natives of Easter Island when they first saw a camera: All they could see was the flash, and, understanding things according to their myths and teachings, they thought the flash was the work of powerful spirits. They could not guess at the mundane reality, that it was the work of Bell and Howell.

Sophisticated Americans too have their myths. One is that all politics is blue smoke and mirrors. Another is that substance, to the common man, is boring, and as Reagan was rarely boring, it follows that he was rarely substantive. Another is that speeches have magical abilities to fool and gull.

My advice to you is: Don't be sophisticated. Be commonsensical. *Speeches actually have to say things. And great speeches are great because they say great things.* Speeches that consist merely of the stringing together of pretty words and pretty sentiments are not great, and never live.

THERE IS NO GREAT SPEECH WITHOUT GREAT POLICY

This is the most important thing a political speechwriter can know, but for everyone else it's important too.

No speech is big without big policy to talk about. Trying to write a great speech without having great policy to work with, to assert and argue for, would be like trying to write a great play about nothing. Great plays are about something, great essays have meaning, and great speeches do, too. The meaning is found in the policy that is being explained and advanced.

Let's look at Lincoln's first inaugural. It was great, but not because he said things in a beautiful way. It was great because he said big, important things, and also said them beautifully.

He explained why, in his view, civil war was threatened; he argued against the war, saying it was unjustified and unlawful; he asserted that he was and must be prepared to resist those who would attempt to secede from the Union; he asked those who would secede and bring war to cease their efforts and remember all that unites us.

His policy was clear: He would work to forestall or avert war, he would fight it if forced. Implicit in his tone was the unstated assertion that if he fought, he would win.

That was his policy. It was expressed almost in the style of a legal brief, or a well-spoken summation to a jury. His words were clear, weighted, at times almost conversational. And there were, this being Lincoln, phrases that entered the national consciousness the moment he spoke them, and that live there still: "the mystic chords of memory," "the better angels of our nature," "we are not enemies but friends."

But the speech wasn't great because of those fine phrases. It was great because his policy was great.

John Kennedy's inaugural was great because it said two big important things. First, he made clear the commitment of his new government to protect political liberty and democratic freedoms throughout the world in the face of what appeared to be growing belligerence on the part of the Kremlin. (This was, obviously, serious policy with worldwide implications.) Second, he asserted that much in our country was about to change because now it was to be led by the junior officers of World War II, who had come of age and come to power with new attitudes and different experiences than their elders. ("The junior officers of World War II" is Theodore H. White's felicitous phrase; as he listened to Kennedy that day he realized the young men who'd fought the war under Eisenhower, the departing president, had now risen to take the old general's place.)

Kennedy made his resolve regarding democratic freedoms clear in a number of passages, including, most famously, the statement, "We will pay any price, bear any burden, suffer any hardship, support any friend and oppose any foe to ensure the survival and success of liberty."

He made the second point clear in a number of passages including the stark and beautiful "Let the word go forth from this time and place, to friend and foe alike, that the torch has been passed to a new generation of Americans—born in this century, tempered by war, disciplined by a hard and bitter peace...."

William Safire has noted that Kennedy adopted the cadences of Lincoln, and followed him in the use of quotation from both the Old and New Testaments.

Kennedy's speech was a marriage of style and substance, and has come to set the standard for modern inaugurals.

It is odd that current political figures, whom you would think (or at least hope) exist for big ideas and serious proposals, are often the first to forget that a great speech must say great things, that it must contain serious policy. They often think style can take the place of substance. They are wrong.

Style enhances substance; it gives substance voice, it makes a message memorable, it makes policy clear and understandable. But it is not itself the message. *Style is not a replacement for substance, and cannot camouflage a lack of substance.*

And where there is no substance, the style will perish. You cannot be eloquent about nothing. You cannot say something banal in a truly interesting way. There are only so many ways to say "Pass the butter," and the more ornate and highly stylized you get—"How I desire to have within my grasp the yellow fatted food that so complements the taste of bread"—the more foolish you'll sound. Because you're only saying pass the butter, which isn't a big thing to say.

What happens if you cannot decide on the substance of your speech—that is, if you don't know what you want to say—but try, anyway, to say it with style?

You fail.

You get Bill Clinton's universally panned second inaugural.

Why was it panned far and wide? Because it actually made

history by being the first inaugural address that was about nothing.

Clinton, as we all know, was from boyhood inspired by JFK. And I think his problem, as he worked on both his first and second inaugurals, may have been that he misunderstood JFK's inaugural. Clinton may have experienced that speech—he was only a boy when he first heard it—as a collection of grand words and singing phrases and ask-nots. He may not have realized that those words and phrases said important and interesting things.

And Clinton, who can be very effective ad-libbing on the stump, is less so in more formal settings. He seems to freeze in formality, losing the almost dangerous looseness that makes him interesting elsewhere. Formal speeches demand sustained seriousness, and one senses with Clinton that he judges himself to be more emotional than cerebral, that he thinks sustained seriousness is simply not his style. Robert Reich, in his affectionate memoir of his tenure as Clinton's Labor secretary, made an observation that may explain some of Clinton's fluidity in informal speeches and tendency to freeze in formal ones. "He was in one of his discursive moods," wrote Reich of a meeting with Clinton. "The very act of talking seems to reassure him that he has a core set of principles." Perhaps reading from a prepared text underscores for him some sense of falsity.

Clinton began with "My fellow citizens," and then said:

> At this last presidential inauguration of the twentieth century, let us lift our eyes toward the challenges that await us in the next century. It is our great good fortune that time and chance have put us not only on the edge of a new century, in

a new millennium, but on the edge of a bright new prospect in human affairs, a moment that will define our course and our character for decades to come. We must keep our old democracy forever young. Guided by the ancient vision of a promised land, let us set our sights upon a land of new promise.

This is one of those paragraphs that makes listeners think, Uh-oh. The self-conscious oratory, the florid phrases, seem unconnected to any specific point.

And then you think: Give him a break, I'm sure he'll explain how this moment in time is going to define our character and how we can keep democracy forever young.

Clinton then quickly reviewed American history and came, within three paragraphs, to the twentieth:

Along the way, Americans produced the great middle class and security in old age, built unrivaled centers of learning and opened public schools to all, split the atom and explored the heavens, invented the computer and the microchip, and deepened the wellsprings of justice by making a revolution in civil rights for African-Americans and all minorities and extending the circle of citizenship, opportunity and dignity to women.

Uh oh. This is not only kind of boring—we've heard this sort of thing, and heard it, and heard it—but you're starting to realize that you are not in good hands. You realize this because he's giving himself the kind of sentences politicians wind up with when they let everyone in the editing process put in a thought—"Don't forget to put in women!" And because he's demonstrating a kind of tin ear. *Microchips?*

Then:

At the dawn of the twenty-first century, a free people must choose to shape the forces of the information age and the global society to unleash the limitless potential of all our people and form a more perfect Union.

Final big uh-oh: *This means nothing.* And we're already well into the speech.

On it went to the end:

> ... by our dreams and labors we will redeem the promise of America in the twenty-first century ... let us meet them with faith and courage ... let us shape the hope of this day ... let us build our bridge. ... May those generations whose faces we cannot yet see, whose names we may never know, say of us here that we led our beloved land into a new century with the American dream alive for all her children, with the American promise of a more perfect Union a reality for all her people, with America's bright flame of freedom spreading. ...

A cavalcade of clichés. But the problem was not that it was written badly. It was thought badly. No one left the Capitol that day knowing what Clinton had said, as they knew what Lincoln had said, and Kennedy, and FDR, and Reagan.

Clinton himself didn't seem to know what he wanted to say in his speech. Perhaps he calculated that if he just said sort of pretty phrases it would sound as if he were communicating big thoughts. But he wasn't. And so his speech will be little noted and not long remembered. This is unfortunate, because every inaugural address is an opportunity to locate and define the truth, or a truth, of one's age. Which is, among other things, a public service.

*   *   *

Remember the stern teacher you had in the fifth grade who
tapped her number-two pencil on the desk, looked at you
dead-eyed and said, "Mr. Smith in the third row: If you have
nothing to say, say nothing"?

This applies to speeches, too.

Don't stand up to speak unless you have something to say
that's worth hearing.

Sometimes in the crush of events or the demands of the
moment the idea of what a speech is about—of what the
implicit or explicit policy is—can be lost. If you are lucky, it
can be retrieved.

A story.

One cool spring day in 1986 I was talking on the phone at
my desk in the Old Executive Office Building, where President Reagan's speechwriters had their offices. Suddenly the
secretary of my boss, the speechwriter Ben Elliott, ran in. "The
Challenger blew up," she said. I looked at the screen of the TV
on a console a few feet away. It was on CNN, no volume. Just
the picture of a cord of white smoke, jaggedly broken against
a perfect blue sky. Pieces of something were falling through
the sky. I stared and thought: What am I looking at? I turned
to Ben's assistant. Behind her now was Ben's eight-year-old
daughter, who had accompanied her father to work that day.
"The teacher is on it," she said. "Is the teacher all right?"

I thought what everyone thought that day: This is impossible. This doesn't happen. The astronauts must have jetti-
soned, separated from the rocket as it began to malfunction.
Why isn't the screen showing a capsule with a parachute float-
ing gently into the ocean? Maybe it's already there, bobbing,
and helicopters are on their way.

Nobody knows. The TV guys don't know. The spokesman

for the mission doesn't know, there's silence on the speaker, you can hear it buzz. The people watching in the stands at the Cape—oh my God, there's Christa McAuliffe's parents, her mother is crying.

Those first minutes, people breathed deep. They breathed deep and took refuge in what they did for a living. The TV people talked, reporters took notes, NASA people made decisions. I turned to my word processor and thought: The president will speak. Whatever happens, however this turns out, the president will make an address. He's in a meeting now, he's with the network anchors—the State of the Union is tonight, he's telling them what points he will emphasize and how he is thinking.

But sooner or later he'll have to speak about this.

I get on the phone. Who has seen the president, what is he saying, is he talking to NASA, what's the state of things? Calls start coming in to my office. One says, every child in the country was watching the liftoff, they were watching in schools across the country. Another says: I was with the president when he got the news, I took notes on what he said. He spoke of the sacrifice of the families of the people on board. He was asked if it was right to have a citizen on board and he said, They're all citizens. He said, This is the last frontier, the most important, and we've become so confident that this is a shock . . . it's traumatic. . . . He was asked if he took any comfort in the fact that we have not lost as many astronauts as the Soviets have in their space program. He shook it off: Sure we take pride in that, but it doesn't lessen our grief. He was asked, What can you say to children to help them understand? He answered, Pioneers have always given their lives on the frontier. The problem is it's more of a shock to all as we see it happening, not just hear about something miles away—but we must make it clear to the children that life goes on. . . .

*   *   *

I realize: That's the speech.

Thinking typing writing thinking. I'm trying to concentrate, the phone is ringing, directives are coming in. Write, rewrite. What's needed, what's not working? It's not enough to say you're sad, not enough to say that they were heroes. The policy—the bed on which the speech rests, the road on which it walks. *The policy*. What would Reagan's policy be? Well, it would be this: A terrible thing has happened but it changes nothing, our resolve continues, we will continue to push on into space. That is our policy: *Nothing ends here.*

Now: What does the speech have to do? What is its job?

- It has to pay honor to the dead, who deserve to be honored.

- It has to reassure the American people that the tragedy, though terrible, will not halt our efforts in space.

- It must tell the world the same. The Cold War is still on and the explosion will be seen to an extent as an international setback; the Soviets will likely use it for their purposes. The world, then, must be told that our resolve continues.

- It has to talk to children about the meaning of the tragedy, and put it into a context they will understand.

A call from the West Wing tells me the president will speak when the search is suspended, they don't know when that will be, they need the speech quick and it should run no longer than five minutes.

Typing thinking writing typing. On TV they keep running the tape of the explosion. Then they go back to the tape from early this morning, when the *Challenger* crew waved goodbye to the cameras as they left to go aboard the shuttle.

As I worked I remembered something, a poem they'd taught us in school, a lovely lyric poem by a flyer named John Gillespie Magee, Jr. It was called "High Flight." It was about the joy of flying, of being liberated from the heavy hand of gravity. And I knew as it came to me that Reagan knew that poem—it had been popular in World War II, flyboys carried copies of it in their wallets. I used it, knowing if Reagan was happy with it he'd keep it and if not it could be cleanly dropped.

I finished, the speech went through staffing, then it went to the president, who edited it. Soon NASA announced what for a few hours had seemed clear: There would be no survivors.

The president went on the air.

Ladies and gentlemen, I had planned to speak to you tonight to report on the State of the Union, but the events of earlier today have led me to change those plans. Today is a day for mourning and remembering.

Nancy and I are pained to the core by the tragedy of the shuttle *Challenger*. We know we share this pain with all of the people of our country. This is truly a national loss.

Nineteen years ago almost to the day, we lost three astronauts in a terrible accident on the ground. But we have never lost an astronaut in flight. We have never had a tragedy like this. And perhaps we have forgotten the courage it took for the crew of the shuttle. But they, the Challenger Seven, were aware of the dangers—and overcame them, and did their jobs brilliantly.

We mourn seven heroes—Michael Smith, Dick Scobee, Judith Resnik, Ronald McNair, Ellison Onizuka, Gregory Jarvis, and

Christa McAuliffe. We mourn their loss as a nation, together.

To the families of the seven: We cannot bear, as you do, the full impact of this tragedy—but we feel the loss, and we are thinking about you so very much. Your loved ones were daring and brave and they had that special grace, that special spirit that says, Give me the challenge and I'll meet it with joy. They had a hunger to explore the universe and discover its truths. They wished to serve and they did—they served us all.

And I want to say something to the schoolchildren of America, who were watching the live coverage of the shuttle's takeoff. I know it's hard to understand, but sometimes painful things like this happen. It's all part of the process of exploration and discovery; it's all part of taking a chance and expanding man's horizons. The future doesn't belong to the fainthearted, it belongs to the brave. The *Challenger* crew was pulling us into the future—and we'll continue to follow them.

I've always had great faith in and respect for our space program—and what happened today does nothing to diminish it. We don't hide our space program, we don't keep secrets and cover things up, we do it all up front and in public. That's the way freedom is, and we wouldn't change it for a minute.

We'll continue our quest in space. There will be more shuttle flights and more shuttle crews and, yes, more volunteers, more civilians, more teachers in space. Nothing ends here—our hopes and our journeys continue.

I want to add that I wish I could talk to every man and woman who works for NASA or who worked on this mission and tell them: Your dedication and professionalism have moved and impressed us for decades, and we know of your anguish. We share it.

There's a coincidence today. On this day 390 years ago the great explorer Sir Francis Drake died aboard ship off the coast of Panama. In his lifetime the great frontiers were the oceans. And a historian later said, "He lived by the sea, died on it, and was buried in it." Today we can say of the *Challenger* crew: Their dedication was, like Drake's, complete.

The crew of the space shuttle *Challenger* honored us by the manner in which they lived their lives. We will never forget them, nor the last time we saw them—this morning, as they prepared for their journey, and waved goodbye, and "slipped the surly bonds of earth" to "touch the face of God."

The president looked so sad. We all were. He had not thought the speech a success, and neither had I by the end, but soon it was called that, I think because it did its job. It made clear the president's policy.

There was almost a last-minute hitch when an NSC staffer decided we had to change the quote in the Magee poem to "reach out and touch someone—touch the face of God." He thought this was eloquent, for he had heard it on TV. We fought him off, but it gave me the willies. Watch out for those who experience eloquence in television commercials.

The president called the next day and asked how I knew he knew the Magee. I didn't, I said, I had a hunch. He told me that the poem was written on a plaque outside his daughter Patti's grade school. He used to see it when he'd pick her up from school.

A few days later I got a letter from someone, a citizen who had written a poem about the *Challenger* and wanted us to see it. It ended, "They left us looking heavenward." To this day I wish that unknown American poet had been in Speechwriting that day.

GIMME ONE A THEM SOUND BITE THINGS

When you work for or with people who have a certain amount of what is called media savvy, you will usually find that they are not only familiar with some of the more wicked clichés of communication, but believe in them. Twenty years ago such people were saying, "The medium is the message." Now they are saying, "It's all sound bites."

It is not all sound bites. And you, as a writer for yourself or others, must never, ever try to write one.

I will tell you why. We will begin with some history.

The "sound bite," as you know, is the little snippet of videotape that television news shows use when they show a politician talking, or a witness describing the crime, or a lawyer insisting on his client's innocence. It's the "bite" of tape the anchorman or reporter "reads into." Dan Rather will begin his broadcast saying, "Great Britain picked a new prime minister today, and when the voting was over a triumphant Tony Blair told supporters a new age had begun." And this will be followed by tape of Blair speaking, a few hours earlier, to a crowd: "I promise you a new Britain, a new spirit, a new beginning—all together now, we'll celebrate tonight but the work begins tomorrow."

What Blair said is the sound bite. Like most politicians today, he probably feels like a walking sound bite.

The term *sound bite* was not commonly used in electronic journalism until the late 1960s and early '70s. That is when the piece of tape used in news reports started to shrink from thirty or forty-five seconds in length to ten or five seconds. Why the shrinkage? Because it was at this time that the owners of networks and local stations began to see that news shows were not only a public service and a prestige item, but a rich potential source of new revenue. News could be profitable. Suddenly networks and local channels were competing against each other in a new way. Where once they competed to get the big stories and get them first, now they competed to have the most popular news show—and charge the highest advertising rates.

Network and local station owners hired legions of media-consulting firms to come in and advise them on how to make their news shows number one in their market. The media consultants told them: Make the news move more quickly, make the stories shorter, include lots of film and tape of action stories—flames licking the sky, sirens, crime scenes with sobbing relatives. *Keep it moving.* Make news more local, they said, more immediately responsive to the needs and lives of the people who watch. (That is how they talk. No one wants to make a living saying, "Make your product glitzier and dumber.") In time the consultants even dictated who would deliver the news— not old graybeard reporters from the wire services but brisk young blondes in Eyewitness News Team Five Live blazers; the consultants even advised dual anchors, so that the studio camera shot would keep moving from one to the other and viewers would be glued to the screen by an unconscious curiosity regarding the level of friendship, or enmity, between Chuck and Sue or Ernie and Roz.

This is how the forty-two seconds of tape of President Eisenhower discussing his budget before the U.S. Chamber of Commerce became the six seconds of tape of President Reagan
addressing the Chamber of Commerce. National politics, it
was judged, was not of local concern. And politicians talk too
long anyway. *Keep it moving.* Cut the president short.

Reagan himself was both amused and frustrated. Once in
his office discussing a speech he looked up and said, "You
know, I'm going to give this whole long speech but they're
going to show two seconds of me, and then Lesley Stahl's
gonna stand there giving her version of what I said with me
going like this"—he moved his mouth vigorously and
silently—"in the background." (Why would networks cut the
president to give more time to the correspondent? Because
when news shows began to compete for popularity, reporters
were promoted as stars; they came to have real marquee value,
and so market value, to the networks. And they lasted: Presidents come and go, but Sam Donaldson is forever.)

Politicians and political speechwriters grew frustrated.
They knew most Americans get their news from TV, but they
knew also there was nothing they could do to improve the situation and get more TV time. Even the TV producers' hands
were tied: They couldn't buck the news director, the news
director couldn't buck the station manager, the station manager couldn't buck the owner, the owner was in the thrall of
the consultants. Sound bites, especially political sound bites,
must be short. (The owners believed the consultants, by the
way, because the consultants' advice seemed to work. Ratings
for Newscenter Four and Eyewitness News and Live at Five
went up. So did the network numbers.)

People in politics kept the new reality in mind and learned
to live with it, as Reagan did. I used to write speeches and then

look at them as a producer would and try to guess what they'd choose for the sound bite. If a sentence jumped out at me and I thought, "That's good, it contains the essence of what he's saying," I'd make sure that it ended a paragraph or started one, so that when producers got the written transcript of the speech before it was delivered they'd be more likely to notice it, underline it, listen for it. If I saw a sentence that I thought producers might like, but I didn't want them to choose it because it didn't communicate the nub of anything, or was only part of a larger argument, I'd make sure it was surrounded by sentences and therefore less noticeable.

You may ask, Why didn't you just set out to write a sound bite and write a good one? And the answer is, I certainly would have if I could have, *but I couldn't.* And I don't think anyone else can, either. It would be like being a songwriter and trying to write a great five-second section of a song. If you obsess on five seconds the song will suffer, it will be oddly shaped, it won't be any good. And even if you succeeded in writing a good five seconds it would be swamped by the surrounding mediocrity of the song. It wouldn't work.

More on that, as they say, in a minute.

In time, sound bites—the word, and what the word meant—became famous. By the late eighties, almost twenty years into the sound bite era, political professionals—pollsters, campaign managers, operatives—were giving print reporters interviews at lunch in which they bragged, "We're winning because we have the best sound bites!" The reporters would leave lunch and write stories: "Think the level of political discourse can't get any lower? Think again. Political insiders in both parties are crowing about their latest attempt to manipulate the media—the Rise of the Sound bite. It's just the latest example of—and encourager of—the dumbing down of politics. And it's working."

Thus was a cliché born. Bright people read about it in the *Washington Post.* Bright producers—the sound bite cutters! the unacknowledged legislators of our age!—read about it, looked at each other in the newsroom, and said, "Do you believe how cynical these politicians are?"

Candidates' wives read the sound bite stories, their children read them, and they called Dad in the Senate cloakroom. Word, too, spread to the corporate suite, the union leader's office. Demand built. The cry filled the air: *Gimme one a them sound bite things!*

By the end of the eighties it got so awful that speechwriters were no longer writing speeches (or were no longer allowed to). Now they were just trying to write one sound bite after another and string them together in hopes that if a television producer didn't like this one he'd like that. Speeches became even less coherent, less interesting, less—worthy. (Did you ever listen to a Bob Dole speech in the '96 presidential campaign? They were one sound bite—or as they used to be called in the speechwriting dodge, one applause line—after another. As in, "There'll be no more crime in a Dole administration." Applause. "And we'll make sure we work hard to put criminals back in jail when you elect us on Tuesday." Applause. Boy, it was awful. Clinton was a little better because he likes to wing it on the stump; you listened, thinking he might say something interesting.)

Soon politicians felt constricted again: "Why does it all have to come down to a snappy line?"

Producers were frustrated: "Why is this all so boring, so predictable and insubstantial?"

Viewers—constituents, voters, people who think—were exasperated: "All of these candidates are so boring and stupid—and they think I'm going to be impressed by sound bites when I want thought and leadership!"

Is there hope? I think so.

First, because things have gotten just about as bad as they can get. And second, because there are answers in history.

What is now called a sound bite was once called a "sentence" or "paragraph" or "phrase." Great sound bites of political history are great *sentences* and *phrases* of political history:

"Gentlemen may cry peace, peace, but there is no peace."

"With malice toward none, with charity for all . . . "

"I have nothing to offer but blood, toil, tears and sweat."

"We have nothing to fear but fear itself."

Those are four of a hundred that would come to mind if you sat down and thought for an hour or two.

They were all created—they came to live in history—because their writers weren't trying to write "a sound bite" or "a line." They weren't trying to self-consciously fashion a phrase that would grab the listener. *They were simply trying to capture in words the essence of the thought they wished to communicate.* And because some of their phrases and sentences were happily brief they wound up in newspaper headlines and in subheads: IN BUOYANT CEREMONY NEW PRESIDENT DECLARES "NOTHING TO FEAR BUT FEAR." Headlines and subheads were the sound bites of yesterday.

In Patrick Henry's case he was trying to say: We must finally admit that war is not only inevitable, it has in fact begun. In Churchill's it was: Our resolve will see us through this darkness. In FDR's: Buck up, in times like this attitude is everything.

All of the famous phrases that came from these thoughts are ringing and memorable because they are natural. That is, they bubbled up from the creative process, they naturally emerged from the process of thinking and writing. They were a thought that emerged in a certain form from a sea of ideas, words, thoughts. *They authentically emerged from thought.*

Lincoln, when he wrote, "With malice toward none ... " was not trying to write a sound bite—though that would have been the great sound bite from his second inaugural. He was trying, simply, to put into words his attitude toward all the people of a broken country as the end of the war approached. He wasn't trying to write a "line"—he was trying to give voice to serious thought and serious policy.

When Ted Sorenson and John Kennedy were working on JFK's inaugural, I am sure they did not think to themselves that "The torch has been passed to a new generation of Americans" was a great sound bite—although it became one of the most famous sound bites of the century. I am sure they thought, instead, that they had created a ringing passage in an elegant speech, a passage that effectively and memorably trumpeted a truth: that the tone and style of American leadership was about to change.

They were serious.

You must be serious when you're doing serious work.

So don't "try to write a sound bite" when you write a speech. Don't try to come up with a great line. Try to write well. Which means, try to think well. Try to put clearly the position you're advancing or the thought you're explaining. Try to explain why your policy is the best one, your attitude the right one, your program the more just one. *Lose yourself in the work and the words will come.*

Think. Try to take the abstract and make it concrete, as Churchill did when he wanted to talk about how Europe, with many in the West barely noticing, had become, at the end of the war, utterly divided. He could have simply said that, and it would have been fine. But he wanted to break through to people with an image; he wanted to make them see what he was talking about. And so he said, "An iron curtain has descended across the continent." A great image because a truthful one, and it has lived for fifty years.

It was also a great sound bite.

But he wasn't trying to write a sound bite.

He was trying to express a thought.

Which is what writers do.

And what you must do.

And, if you are in politics, take comfort in this. When the age of the sound bite began there were no alternatives on television to the evening news shows. The networks had information hegemony. But, as you know, a small minority of Americans now get all their news from Dan Rather and Peter Jennings, or Chuck and Sue. There is news all over the place now. You can watch complete speech after complete speech on C-Span and C-Span 2. You can hear long sections of speeches on radio shows, on Rush Limbaugh's and others. You can watch long speeches live from the floor of the House and the Senate. There is a greater demand for serious, thoughtful, porous, textured speeches than ever.

Television producers are still the unacknowledged legislators of the world (as Shelley said of poets) but there are more of them, in more venues, and their jobs have in some ways changed. For one thing, they're all tired of sound bites. They'd be relieved to run longer sections of a speech—six or seven sentences! In the past few years there has been a greater media self-consciousness about running short sound bites; there's a movement to make them longer.

But even if that were not true, the larger point remains: If

you try to write a sound bite you will not write a good one, and
so you will defeat your purpose. But if you try to express a
thought in an interesting way, if you seriously try to communicate an interesting viewpoint or assert an interesting fact, you
will more likely succeed. And write an interesting section of a
speech. Which becomes a sound bite.

Try to think clearly and write well. Leave the sound bite to
God.

Once, years ago, when I was new to Washington, I was sitting
with friends and we were talking about politics when I put
forth an opinion, made some observation about the political
scene. And one of the men with us, a political activist, nodded
and said, approvingly, "That's a good line." I blinked, sort of
confusedly perturbed. I had been complimented in a way that
was diminishing. An older gentleman who was with us looked
at the fellow and said, "Actually, it was a thought." He looked
at me and nodded. "It was a good thought."

It gave me an insight into how political people view a
thought that is compactly expressed. They think it is a line, a
thing to be used for gain in argument or debate.

We must ignore these people, while acknowledging that they
exist and, among political, media and business folk, predominate.

SOUND BITE II, THE SEQUEL

It is not only in speeches that the quest for the sound bite has become a problem.

In 1984, when Walter Mondale was running for the Democratic nomination for president, he appeared in a debate with Gary Hart and issued forth a celebrated sound bite. Hart had been talking about his positions and plans when Mondale leaned forward and interrupted him with the words, "When I hear your new ideas, I'm reminded of the ad, 'Where's the beef?'"

The crowd roared, no doubt partly from surprise, for Mondale had not been known for apt cultural references. It was an important moment for him. It not only made him seem like something more interesting than a large beige blur, it shrewdly targeted a weakness many Democrats were beginning to perceive in Hart's candidacy. What exactly were his policies? Did he really have ideas, or only an interesting persona and a great jawline?

It later came out—it always comes out—that Mondale had been given the line in the car on the way to the debate by a bright young aide who explained it to him. "Where's the beef?" was the question asked by a nice old lady in a popular television commercial for the hamburger chain Wendy's. It meant, Sure McDonald's has flash and dash and arches, but they don't have a lot of meat in their burgers. They don't have a lot of substance inside that great packaging.

After the success of Mondale's line, the word went forth: Candidates needed to be supplied by their staff with zippy sound bites before they went into a debate or an interview.

And this is still the reigning cliché.

Now, I am not going to decry its wickedness. I am not even going to suggest that it is new. FDR's aides gave him the bright suggestion that he deny he was in Philadelphia when asked by the press why he had not delivered on a campaign pledge made in Philadelphia in the previous campaign. Aides are always giving candidates lines, and always have.

Now it is simply more so. But I think candidates and campaign aides should try to remember this: We are decades into the age of the sound bite and thirteen years from Mondale's great moment. In that time the American public has become very sophisticated about such lines, so sophisticated that they now discount them. If I were advising a candidate, I would say, "Don't be so eager to be bright and quick and clever and memorable. Be you, try to be honest, speak with all the candor you can muster and say it the way you'd say it to your family."

Otherwise, oddly enough, you'll bore everybody.

You could start a new trend called, perhaps, ingenuousness. It could really take off and, as it spread, produce a new and nonwicked reigning cliché.

WRITING SPEECHES FOR OTHER PEOPLE

YOU HAVE TO FIND THEIR SOUND

If you write speeches for a business leader, a CEO, the head of an organization or a political figure, you face a special challenge. You have to do everything you would do to write a speech for yourself, plus one more thing. You have to find the voice of the person you're writing for.

Finding that voice can be hard. But there are things to look for to help you. Everyone has a different way of speaking—different rhythms to their speech, different words they tend to use. They have their own vocabulary. They have the kind of references they would use to make a point. One person might say, "My mother always told me . . . " Another, "As T.S. Eliot said . . . " Another, "Remember Don Corleone? 'It was Barzini all along.'" Another, "I was talking to Marianne the other day and I had this thought."

You have to listen for how people speak, the words they use and how they use them. You have to listen, too, for how they think—in a concrete and linear way, for instance, or a circular and abstract way. Some people have a thinking and speaking style that is logical, linear, point by point. Some are intuitive and make odd but often apt comparisons, sometimes using interesting images. Some people are witty and some are comical and some are neither, or neither very much.

Most of us are some combination of some or all of these things.

Some people speak in long and graceful paragraphs that introduce a subject, play with it, question whether it is the right thing to be discussed, decide that it is, and explore it. Some people speak in short bursts of information followed by silence. The silence may be long or short.

The way people speak usually reflects how they think. And so you must listen closely, not only so that the work you do sounds like them, but so it sounds like them thinking.

To a degree this requires a talent that is simply natural, and therefore unteachable.

Sometimes you can find a person's voice in the things they've written. You can discover how they think, too. When you read the writings of the pope, in spite of the fact that you are probably reading a translated document, you can still hear the pope's voice. It is gentle and rounded, not sharp edged. It's soft and circular but it has weight, it's not light. He has a way of introducing a subject, circling around it, leaving it and then returning. But when he returns he broadens his point, makes it wider, connects it to other things, and then moves on again. His style, those who know him say, reflects his way of thinking. It is almost a style of thinking. It is, for me, difficult; it demands much of the reader. When I read him, I struggle, but at the end I think: It was worth it. And so I leave fed, and not fatigued.

Richard Nixon, in his public speaking, was logical, linear. He liked to tick off his points one by one as he built his case. "First, the Hanoi government is wrong in its claims. Second, even if they were right what they insist on would still be, for us, impossible. Third . . . " Nixon spoke with unseen colons: "Let me say this about that:" His writers were faithful to his style. Nixon giving a speech was like Nixon in conversation. (Except at the end of his White House years, when we can see in the transcripts of the tapes that anxiety had fractured his coherence.) His writers were faithful to his style not because they had no style of their own to bring—they were Pat Buchanan and William Safire, who had their own strong natural styles that would later be brought to the writing of columns in which their voices were a distinct presence—but because they understood their job was to help Nixon be the best possible Nixon, not a more elderly version of Buchanan or a less humorous version of Safire.

You have to literally be close to someone to get his sound. You have to be exposed to him, sit in his office and hear him talk to you and others, hear him answer the phone and talk about a show that was on TV last night. You have to get to the point that you can hear him in your head.

By the way, if you have any gift at all for mimicry, you probably have a gift for absorbing someone else's sound. If you do a good imitation of your Irish neighbor who speaks with a brogue and who always scratches his right ear when he tells a joke, you're imitating not only his lilt but his syntax, his rhythm, his choice of words, his way of pausing and cocking his head.

Ronald Reagan had a rounded way of speaking. I used to imagine him in my mind as an old sailor, a wise ol' salt ambling down a rolling deck as the ship rolled in the sea. He never fell or had to grab the rails, he just rolled with the swells as they rose and fell. George Bush, on the other hand, was like a man briskly walking down a city sidewalk, stopping all of a sudden to greet a friend and then plowing on, slowing briefly for a light, going forward with the crowd, turning to say hello to the man at the hot dog stand, moving on. Years later, after he'd left the White House, a friend of his said, "Did you ever see George fish? Throws the line in, waits twenty seconds, reels it in, throws it somewhere else, waits twenty seconds. Always thinking, Fish ain't here, maybe there." I thought, Yes—at his best there's an energy and eagerness, at his worst a frantic quality. Reagan, forced to fish, would have cast into deep waters, let the line sit, and waited. While telling stories about waiting: "There was a little boy back where I lived, and he wanted a red sled he'd seen in the window of a department store. Every day he'd go by and stare at it, dreaming . . . "

Bush would have said, "Little boy wanted a sled. Saw it, gotta have it. Couldn't get it out of his head."

Reagan spoke in finished sentences, Bush in bursts. "And I don't *want* broccoli and I'm *the president* and I don't *have* to eat broccoli." You can see in Reagan's letters a fluidity that speaks of serenity. You can see in Bush's a brevity that speaks of movement.

When I worked for them, I kept in mind the different styles of speaking—which reflected in part different ways of thinking—and tried to see that they were reflected in the work. Sometimes it caused problems. In Bush's case, I noticed he often, in conversation, began sentences with "And . . . " So I would keep this in mind and, where I thought he'd begin a sentence with *And,* I'd write *And.* But I was only guessing where he'd say *And.* And often I guessed wrong. He would read the speech, keep my *Ands* and, when he stood to speak, add his *Ands.* The result: He wound up saying *And* too much. Sometimes knowing their style, absorbing it and sending it back to them can pervert their style. And what I did was . . . stop writing *and.*

Bush famously didn't like the first-person pronoun. He was allergic to *I.* So I tried to arrange things so that he didn't have to say *I* a lot. But when I wrote it, and he had okayed it, and edited it, I expected he would say it. He didn't. He'd take the one lone and necessary *I* right out. So I started putting *I*'s back in.

I talked to two highly regarded writers about the challenges they face when they write speeches for others. One of them is Lisa Schiffren, a writer and essayist who was a speechwriter for Dan Quayle and who in fact drafted his famous Murphy Brown speech. Lisa is brilliant, a born observer of herself and others. I've broken what she told me down into short sections and attempted to keep her voice.

LISA

WHEN SHE BEGINS WRITING

First I have grand notions of what is going to happen, the high-blown phrases that you think of while you're walking around or taking a shower. But the truth is, you have to begin with the hard and sometimes boring work of looking over whatever it is the person you're writing for has sent you—previous speeches, government research, or in the case of businessmen the annual report, the company propaganda. And you read it. And then you talk to the person and get some notion of what they have in mind. "What do you want to say in this speech, what do you want to communicate?"

I wish I could write out an outline in linear form, with roman numerals and sub-points. But after the research I just start typing as fast as I can all of the things that are in my head—serious points and serious phrases. A lot of this stuff, half of it, you'll lose.

If your training is legal or in terms of writing memos, you'll do the logic and then add the flourishes later. But I do the flourishes and add the logic later.

But taking notes of what you want to include—a three-point note to yourself to tell people what you're going to say in the opening, describe the problem at whatever length is appropriate, and then describe the solution—that's fine.

What Lisa says here I've found to be true for most speechwriters, and most writers. I've never known a good writer who used a formal outline, ever. The reason, I suppose, is that writing is a creative act and creativity by its nature does not lend itself to point-by-point directives. Creativity is an unbounding; you don't want to tie yourself down. If you were a professional car driver and you were given a map to a place and told you must not deviate from the route laid out . . . you'd get bored. You wouldn't be able to pull off a reliable but dull highway and find your own way, which might get you to the destination quicker and with a better view. Sticking with the assigned route will probably get you where you're going, but it may make you fall asleep at the wheel, and make your passengers fall asleep, too.

WATCH OUT FOR IRONY

Things like sarcasm and irony, which intellectuals find so charming, really should never be used in public. They depend so much on nuance and inflection, and more people than you would imagine will miss it.

WORKING ON THE VOICE

If you're writing for somebody you know and with whom you have an ongoing relationship, which is ideal, it's easier to write for them because you've listened to them with your inner ear—you have absorbed their cadences, the phrases that work for them. This is important. You could write the same speech on welfare in terms of substance for Dan Quayle and Phil Gramm, but not in terms of style.

Hearing them—listening to them closely and being able to really hear how they speak—is simply an intuitive process. It can't be taught.

Here's something you can do to check. Read it aloud. If you're writing for Newt Gingrich, write a section and read it aloud. Can you "hear" Newt reading it? Or are you hearing somebody else, anybody else, you?

When you type up your notes on points to be made—that's the point at which you start reading sentences aloud.

You learn two things from this exercise. One is if the speech works in terms of oral ability—if the sentences are too long and impossible to say, if it reads well but doesn't speak well. And two, that's when you can start to figure out if the speech is starting to sound like the guy you're writing for. That's when you think maybe a Shelby Steele would use this phrase, but Dan Quayle shouldn't use this phrase.

YOU HAVE TO BE TOUGH

You want to consider the person you're writing for ruthlessly. Is this somebody who's aloof and needs to be warmed up with a piece of homey phrasing, or whatever? Is it someone who could surprise an audience by using very clear and analytic language?

But whatever moderating stylistic device, it will only work if it's plausible, if it's true of them or true of some facet of them.

WHEN YOU'RE DONE WITH THE SPEECH

Here's what always happens. You've read what they've given you, you've talked to them about what they want to say, you've thought about how to synthesize all the data, you've written the speech they said they want, you give it to them, and here's what always happens:

They look at it . . . and only then do they focus. The tactile fact of holding it in their hand and reading it with their eyes produces the moment at which they decide what it is they want. This, in my experience, is universal. It's a prolonged or extended version of what happens when you go shopping. You want a black dress with a V neck. But you go to the stores, go through the racks, and you never walk out with what you wanted. You looked and changed your mind.

A politician tells you he wants a duck. Then he looks at it and says, "Uhhh, I wanted a chicken." He's thinking, It's poultry, it's related. But it's not what he asked for.

Or another version: He tells you what he wants, you take careful notes, you organize the material, you put it into his language, you know you captured both him and his thoughts, and you give it to him . . . and he is disappointed. Why? Because it sounds just like him!

He wanted to sound better. In fact he does, but he can't tell. In fact, he wanted to sound like someone else, and thought it was your job to make him into someone else! He thinks you didn't do any work! He thinks you just wrote what he told you!

And so he's disappointed.

And what you do in all these cases is . . . go back to the computer. Rewrite.

WATCH OUT FOR BOSSES WHO SAY "GO DO YOUR MAGIC"

It's their way of saying, "I could do magic but I'm a serious person doing serious things." It's their way of saying, "It better be good." It's their way of saying, "Reinvent me." It's their way of saying, "Go utilize your little gift."

You must tell them, seriously: It's not magic, it's hard work.

MAKE THE BOSS PRACTICE

A lot of men who are successful think they've gotten where they've gotten because they're naturals. And they resent the idea that they have to practice something as natural and simple as speaking. But they must.

Inflection is everything. The sense that this text is you and truly reflects you is everything. You have to practice in part so that you can look up as you read and look at the audience and nod and make eye contact for a few seconds. This is interesting because it's natural. Also, you don't want to look like a nerd who's hiding behind a text because he's afraid to look up.

Reagan was the most natural speaker in politics, but he was a natural because he practiced so hard. He's the one who worked and reworked everything and practiced emphasis.

A SMART BUT UNUSUAL WAY TO JUDGE YOUR WORK

An appropriate speech is one that doesn't call particular attention to itself. There's a Coco Chanel story—she said that if a woman walks into a room wearing one of her dresses and everyone says, "What a dress!" then she has failed. But if the woman walks into a room and people say, "Oh, you look fabulous," then she has succeeded.

The speech analogue is this: You want people to say, after hearing you, "She's very intelligent, she made some really interesting points." Not "Oh, what an interesting speech."

For six years Kerry Tymchuk was a speechwriter for Bob Dole, for eight a speechwriter for Elizabeth Dole. Kerry worked the '96 presidential campaign and a few months later talked to me about being a speechwriter in politics. To me, a lot of what distinguishes Kerry is his loyalty to his boss and the fact that he made Bob Dole the object of real study. He bothered to know him. That—and the fact that Dole included him in things in the office, didn't keep him apart, as sometimes happens with speechwriters—is why Kerry's work was good.

Again, a point-by-point version of Kerry's thoughts, in which I tried to preserve his voice.

KERRY

SOMETHING ABOUT SPEECHWRITERS

Something speechwriters share is that we're interested. We watch news, we watch speeches, we listen to speeches.

Over the years I've heard Dole speak countless, countless times. Speechwriters listen not only for what the person is saying but how he's saying it. A lot of it is trial and error. The majority of speeches for Dole were the hybrid speech—the American Home Builders are in town, so he goes to them with talking points, with a lot of room for ad-libbing.

He takes a lot of kidding about referring to himself as Bob Dole. "Bob Dole thinks," "Bob Dole believes." I asked him about it. Some of it was "I don't want to sound like I'm bragging," some of it was "The more I mention the name the more people remember it!"

Dole was known for his wit, but I always think Dole didn't tell jokes—he told truths, but with humor. It's not a good idea to try to be funny if you're not. Dole just naturally was.

What works all the time is self-deprecation. Dole would say things like, "You may be wondering why I was chosen to be your speaker today. It's quite simple. I was the lowest bidder." That was just him.

A KEY TO UNDERSTANDING HIS BOSS

Dole has always had a problem with the theatrics of a speech. He has trouble with artifice. The ironic thing is he has to act every day because he's in pain every day. I think he figured, that's act-ing enough. So why should he have to act and pretend he's not bored when he's bored, or act like he believes something that he doesn't believe?

He's in pain because of his right arm. It hurts every day. It hurts because he doesn't do what others who have been injured as he was injured would do—let the arm hang, in which case the hand would hang limp and splay backwards. The nerves and tendons in it were removed and that's what happens. But instead of just letting it hang, which would be natural and easy, he lifts it up and locks the arm in front of him, grasping the pen in the hand. Some of it is to ward off people from trying to shake his right hand. Some of it is for appearance. But it takes a remarkable amount of strength to keep that arm locked in position when you're in public. And he's always in public.

So it aches. It hurts all the time. The shoulder hurts too. And he acts like it doesn't.

DOLE DETACHES

When Dole gives a speech he's both the speaker and the audience—he listens to what he says and he can't help making comments on it. He's almost winking at the audience.

He's not cynical about America, about patriotism and service to country and veterans. The times he's cried in public over the years, like the Nixon funeral, when people were surprised he cried: A lot of that was patriotism. And a lot of that was that he was thinking he's Bob Dole from Russell, Kansas, giving a eulogy at a presidential funeral—who would have thought it?

The toughest swear word I ever heard him say in six years was *jiminy*. When he's really angry or mad or surprised he'll say, "Jiminy!" There's that surprising innocence.

TEXTUAL DEVIATE

It hurts when Dole doesn't use a line that I know would work. In the convention speech process there was a part of the speech where he talks about America and its ideals. I suggested, "It's these ideals that make America at 220 years the youngest nation on earth—it's these ideals that make me at seventy-three years the youngest man in this hall." And at the end Dole laughed and said, "Strom Thurmond probably thinks he's the youngest man in the hall." And he took it out. It hurt. Those things always hurt.

DOLE GIVES THE RICHARD NIXON EULOGY

Nixon died and the family called the next day. The funeral was set for a few days away. They asked Dole to speak and assigned him a general topic, as they did all the speakers: Kissinger spoke on Nixon and foreign policy, Pete Wilson on Nixon and California, Dole on Nixon the man and the pragmatist, how he got things done.

I met with Dole in his office and he said, "Here's what I'm thinking about." It was a team process, with the writer and Dole adviser Richard Norton Smith, of the Ford Library. We all talked and faxed drafts back and forth to each other. I'd fax one to Dole and he'd make substantial edits and fax it back to me. I said, "Let's use the anecdote about Nixon's last visit to the Capitol last January" (just a few months before he died). Dole hosted a luncheon to mark the twenty-fifth anniversary of Nixon's inauguration. It was in the Mansfield Room of the U.S. Capitol—one hundred guests, including senators, congressmen, and former members who'd served under Nixon.

And at the end of the lunch Nixon got up and without a note in his hand gave one of the most compelling speeches Dole had ever heard—thirty minutes, a tour of the horizon summing up America's future in the next century. You don't get Dole to sit still for thirty minutes, or three minutes for that matter, as a rule. But you could have heard a pin drop during the whole presentation.

So in the eulogy Dole talked about it, the last time he saw the president. And then it continued—Dole told how he took Nixon to his office to rest, but he couldn't rest because pages and tourists, a hundred of them, lined up outside to shake hands, and Nixon shook every last one.

I knew it had to be in the speech. I was at the lunch, watching Dole throughout. I knew how much it meant to him, and how much Nixon did.

It worked because I was there. If I hadn't been there I never would have known.

The speech I'm proudest of was given on Dole's final day in the Senate, the speech from the floor. He had a full text in front of him, but it was definitely a hybrid because he went off, as I knew he would, on his own memories. The strength of that speech came from knowing Dole's history. I knew he'd want to mention Senator Inouye, I knew he'd want to mention Hubert Humphrey.

ADVICE FOR SPEECHWRITERS

I'd just say: Listen. Listen to your boss when he's giving a speech and not giving a speech. Listen to how he talks. Take mental note of what works and what doesn't.

And if you don't respect him you shouldn't be there. How could you work for someone you don't respect as a person and believe in? You don't have to agree with him on every issue, but if you believe in him and you understand why he's taking a position, you can write that position with a clear conscience. But if you don't believe in him . . .

Do you have to be politically, philosophically in tune? You don't have to be in lockstep, but you have to be fairly closely attuned. You have to be true to yourself and true to who you're working for. How can you go to work every day and write what you don't believe in? In the end you'd compromise somewhere—by not really serving your boss, or by compromising your own integrity. There are more important things in life than being true to a senator, and one is being true to yourself. I couldn't work for Ted Kennedy because I don't agree with him.

A word about writing humor in speeches for others.

It can get tricky. When I worked for Vice President Bush, he was sometimes called upon to make funny speeches. But Bush didn't like prepared humor, and he often didn't think jokes that I thought were funny were funny. (It's an odd thing about humor, people react to it in an almost intimate way. "I *love* it!" "I *hate* that!") In 1988, at the Al Smith dinner in New York, a political event at which the Democratic and Republican nominees for president always show up and make a witty speech, I loaded Bush's speech up with every good joke I could get my hands on. I did this because I knew he'd kill half of them, but if he kept half he'd be okay. I also wrote some serious sections, blocks of Bush's thoughts about the campaign and its meaning. But here was my mistake: The serious sections played off of and were thematically connected to the jokes.

Of which Bush killed almost all. Michael Dukakis got up to speak first and he was really good—witty one-liner after one-liner. He was self-deprecating and sly and his jokes were connected to each other; one built on the other. I was in the audience. I listened to the laughter and looked at Bush on the dais. He was furiously scribbling. I began to get the empathetic flop sweat speechwriters get when their guy is about to go down.

I knew Bush had been given jokes by his friends in the past few days and had stuffed them in his pockets. Now he was rooting around in his pockets, taking out pieces of paper and quickly scanning them.

He stood to speak. He kept the serious portions of the speech because he'd liked them. And where I'd written a joke that he had removed, he put in one of the jokes he'd found in his pocket.

Boy, did it not work. It wasn't terrible, it wasn't horrible, but it was second or third rate. Mike Dukakis sat back in his chair on the dais with a smile that was a purr. You could almost see the little canary feathers sticking out of the corners of his mouth.

What I learned was to tell the boss that if he removes the jokes it's fine, but the jokes are connected to the serious sections and if he takes out the one he must take out the other and we must begin again, rewriting top to bottom.

I also learned that candidates—and business leaders—often think that because a speech requires wit it's not a serious or important speech, and so they can be haphazard about it. But every speech a candidate or leader makes is serious and important, because every speech is an opportunity to succeed or fail in front of an audience that just may include the press. So tell the boss before work on the speech begins: This is important, even though it's supposed to make people laugh.

Connected to which, a thought. Actually a wee editorial.

I was struck, in the 1980s, by how often presidents and vice presidents and first ladies and senators had to go out and make funny speeches. It had become a Washington tradition, the Washington Correspondents Association Witty Speech, the Radio and TV Correspondents Witty Speech, the Gridiron Witty Speech, the White House Press Photographers Witty

Speech. The president had become an entertainer. Every month or so it seemed he was going before some group and telling jokes. As if he were Bob Hope or Jay Leno or Rosie O'Donnell.

I thought, once a year is fine, the Al Smith dinner is fine, but this is ridiculous. He's the leader of the United States, he's negotiating START tomorrow, this isn't right. It isn't dignified. It isn't what a serious person does.

But the cliché wisdom within the White House—and it was a wicked (though in its way practical) cliché—was that these were almost uniformly press events, and if you didn't show up the press would beat you up and call you a bad sport and a stiff. They'd make you pay for your absence with negative columns and editorials.

This argument was buttressed by what happened after Nancy Reagan took part in a self-spoofing skit at the annual Gridiron show. It was early in the Reagan presidency, and Mrs. Reagan was under daily fire for Insensitivity at a Time of National Want. The country was in recession and she was buying red china for the White House dinner service (with donated money, it should be noted) and borrowing gowns from designers to wear at state dinners. So she showed up at the Gridiron and made marvelous fun of herself in a skit called "Second Hand Rose," in which she played a scheming materialist who sings such lyrics as "I sure hope Ed Meese sews."

It was a hit. The press corps loved it and roared approval. And they rewarded Mrs. Reagan with a lot of good press. It helped turn her reputation around. The press now felt it wasn't sporting to put her down for sins she'd admitted and even made a song of . . . all for the entertainment of the press.

From then on it was a reigning cliché: Presidents and Vice Presidents and First Ladies Do These Things.

But I'll tell you, it's gotten worse. It's twisted now, and unwell, and the press shouldn't be laughing.

Now Clinton and Gore and senators and ambassadors go before the Alfalfa Club and the rest not to burnish their reputation, but to turn serious scandals into jokes. In the middle of the Chinese influence-peddling scandal a Democratic senator showed up at one of the dinners to speak with a suitcase as a prop, and made jokes about how he is a bagman. The press thought it was really funny. At the May 1997 White House Correspondents Association dinner President Clinton made jokes about the growing fund-raising scandals: For $10,000 you can now meet with Al Gore to discuss reinventing government, "and for $20,000 you don't have to go." *Badaboom.* On the selling of the Lincoln bedroom he said, "The bad news is our only daughter is going off to college. The good news is it opens up another bedroom." That line was one of many of a similar nature.

Senators make jokes about how they break the law, presidents make jokes about the suits brought against them for sexual harassment. The press laughs and later rewards them with sympathetic words in columns and stories.

But the presidents and senators laugh loudest. Because they know that just by showing up and telling their jokes they're getting themselves off the hook.

Intelligent Americans watch, back home, on C-Span. I wonder if they think, as they watch the politician and hear the uproarious laughter of the press corps: I am looking at two halves of a hypocrisy.

For if you step back a minute, as the senators and presidents make their jokes from the podium, you could fairly wonder: *Why is this funny?* If the czar stood up in 1912 and spoke to the Moscow Writers Guild and referred in a self-deprecating fashion to the imperfections of his government—"Sure we killed a few peasants, but the Jews only went to jail!"—would that be funny? Or would we look at those words and that event now and note their decadence, and the writers' complicity in the decadence?

When presidents do stand-up, anything can happen. And when anything can happen, anything will. Don Imus shows up to speak at a dinner and looks over at the sitting president, who smoothly, confidently smiles from the dais, and insults him, using as his material the president's sexual history. This is what Don Rickles used to do to Sammy and Dean used to do to Frank, in Vegas. But is it right—is it good—to do this in public to the man who, whatever his failings, may some day be forced by history to lead our nation through the wreckage of nuclear tragedy?

And why would the president stay and watch as the stature of the presidency was lowered that evening? Does he not know that that diminishing could prove dangerous to others? Doesn't he know that even if it is in part his fault, that he himself has contributed heavily to the loss of the presidency's mystique— doesn't he know that this further diminishing may someday prove harmful to innocent people who are not in a position to be in this room this evening clad in tuxedos and drinking red wine? Who are not caught by the camera laughing in the cut-away shot?

I don't mean to be somber. I don't mean there's no place for humor in politics. I don't mean Don Imus is indefensible. Don Imus is the id of the chattering classes; he gives voice to what some people think and do not say. This may be a public service. And certainly putting our leaders down is an old tradition and a good one. But even Imus knew he'd gone too far, as they say. He gleamed in the lights with a flop sweat so deep and shiny you could have basted a turkey with his forehead. Later he boldfaced it: "It doesn't get any better than this." And in truth it did not hurt him. His defenders said, with some justice, that the organizers of the dinner knew what they were getting when they hired him.

Indeed they did. Just as Clinton knew why he was staying, and not walking off the dais: because he was afraid of headlines that would say, CLINTON STALKS OFF. That would have "looked defensive." The press wouldn't have liked it. They would have punished him.

So he stayed. Almost declaring, by his presence, "You're right, Don, I happen to be an amoral trash-head from shantytown!"

And why shouldn't he say that, directly or indirectly, by his presence? He's just a president. And presidents are guys who do stand-up. And sometimes stand-up, as they used to say, turns blue.

Presidents should stop doing stand-up. It's not their job. The press should stop being impressed by stand-up. It's not their job either. They should all act like grown-ups, and if they're not really grown-ups they should fake it, and stop frightening the children.

Thank you.

Everyone who writes speeches for other people knows the horror of the vetting or editing process. The writer writes, and then the aides of the person for whom the speech has been written descend upon the text to make their changes. This can be frustrating. For one thing, the aides are not usually themselves writers or particularly sensitive to the written word. For another, they are paid to be defensive. It is their job to make sure nothing bad happens, and so they read with an eye to removing potential trouble. But if a speech is shaped, ultimately, by the overwhelming desire that nothing bad happen, then nothing good will happen either. The speech will sound mealy-mouthed and nervous. Also, aides and lawyers are, simply, paid to take things out. Writers are paid to put things in. Aides and lawyers sometimes think the more they remove from a speech, the more they're proving their worth. And finally, most people can't help fiddling with a text. They see themselves as writers because after all they are: They've written letters to their parents, they wrote papers at school. And if they're writers, why can't they rewrite your sorry prose?

There is no absolute protection from this, but there are things you can do to deal with it. The first is to do good work and build up their respect for you. The second is to try to become friends with the aides and lawyers and earn their trust. Most important, you have to become close to—or be perceived to be close to—the person you're writing for. When he says something that you later put in the speech, it can be very helpful to be able to say in the ensuing editing, "You can take that out if you like, but the boss won't be happy because he told me quite specifically to put it in." When they begin to understand that you're writing what the boss is thinking, they'll be more likely to applaud what they previously would have removed.

If a corporate or political speechwriter is reading this right now, he or she may be turning to his or her spouse and saying, "Did I ever tell you about the time they took out the best phrase in a big speech?"

We all have our war stories. Here's one of mine.

Once when I was working for President Reagan, during the 1984 presidential campaign, I was writing a pretty gloves-off, partisan speech for the boss. (Well, about as gloves-off as Reagan got. He was usually gentle with his adversaries, humorous and teasing but never sharp and mean.) I was writing away on some section about the Democratic Congress, and I thought of the liberal congressman Tom Downey. Then I thought of the liberal senator Christopher Dodd. Then I thought of the liberal congressman Norman Dicks. They, I thought, are part of the problem, the reason a popular conservative president can't get the changes he wants through Congress. It's the Downeys, Dicks and Dodds.

All were veteran members and well-known aggressors in the political wars of the day. It struck me that their names were alliterative, and that they went together with a happy and mischievous suggestiveness, as in, "Help me, Doc, I don't know if it's Tourette's syndrome or Downey's Dicksindodds, but it hurts like hell." Individually, as every housewife and some househusbands know, Downey is soft, Dodd sounds doddering and . . . well, when Christine Baranski on *Cybil* refers to her husband as Dr. Dick, it is not a compliment.

Anyway, I thought: Why not use their names to capture for people what is wrong with and must be changed about the United States Congress? It would be like FDR's merry attack on the conservative House members Martin, Barton and Fish, who he felt kept him from making the kind of liberal change he needed to make. He was very funny and very tough with ol' Martin and Barton and Fish.

What "the Downeys, Dicks and Dodds" had was, it was merry. And aggression should always be merry in politics. It would supply our troops with something they could hold on to—"We'd have lower taxes if it weren't for those liberals, those whatchamacallit Downeysdickandodds." It's one thing to rail against the thirty-year-long Democratic control of Congress, another to be able to refer to it with names that personalize the problem.

So I wrote a merrily aggressive speech and threaded their names throughout and had a heck of a lot of fun. And I know Reagan would have loved it if indeed he'd ever seen it.

Which he never did.

Because his top aides had to okay a speech before he saw it and they wouldn't okay it, for one not-so-bad reason and one bad one. The bad reason was that they were afraid of riling the Democrats. They thought that unriled Democrats might give Reagan legislation a fair hearing. This was a wonderful example of what is known as magical thinking. It was comparable to a Dick Gephardt thinking to himself, "Gee, if I'm just careful not to irritate Tom Delay I'm sure he'll stop being a conservative!" Liberals were not going to give Reagan or his legislation a fair hearing because they were liberals; they were philosophically opposed to what he stood for. Why would they change their minds over something as small as stroking or not being stroked?

The not-so-bad reason not to have fun with DD&D was that it would raise Downey, Dick and Dodd to Reagan's level. Reagan only zeroed in on big guys, and this jokey reference would raise their stature and ensure their reelection.

I understood this, but I disagreed with it because (a) it didn't hurt FDR or help Martin, Barton and Fish when he singled them out; FDR didn't fear he was elevating them, he thought he was spoofing them. And (b) Downey, Dicks and Dodd were all solidly popular in their areas, they weren't going away any time soon. But at least now they'd have to go home as poster children for liberalism and have to answer Reagan's derisive sally.

And apart from all that I thought: Hey guys, politics is supposed to be fun. Mix it up.

But it was too colorful and too aggressive for Reagan's vet-ters. And so it was consigned to the round file. And to this day I think: God, that speech would have been good!

By the way, thirteen years later Dodd is still in the Senate. Dicks is still in the House. Downey was defeated in 1992.

It always hurts when things you really like are cut. But you know what's funny? It rarely makes a difference as to how things work out. Scott Fitzgerald said writers scream and kick over edits, but at the end you rarely miss what was removed. It always seems earthshaking, but it never is.

A digression about something I'm often asked.

Whenever I make a speech and talk about speechwriting and politics and communication, almost always someone will stand up and ask, "Why do presidents have speechwriters? Wouldn't it be better and more honest if they did it themselves?"

I answer yes, it would be better, but presidents speak all the time and ultimately they would have to face a choice: I can be president and govern, or I can be a speechwriter and write speeches, but I can't do both.

Presidents speak three and four and five times a day—in the Rose Garden, to small groups in the Roosevelt Room, to federal employees in the State Department, to party activists in the Old Executive Office Building, to intellectuals in the East Room. And those are only the things that the press doesn't cover. The press is there, cameras rolling, for everything else: the short speech in the press room, the opening remarks at the press conference, the announcing of a new initiative.

I would argue that modern presidents speak too much and diminish the importance of their pronouncements by endless jawboning. I think they should be more quiet than they are, and read more.

But even if a new president did half as many speeches as
Bill Clinton, who gives more but not much more than George
Bush, he'd still be speaking a lot. And he would still need
speechwriters. One reason is that a president really can't be
winging it a lot because everything he says—he is, after all, the
leader of the most powerful nation on earth—has implications, sometimes serious ones. A small aside badly phrased can
make the stock market plummet, or give China an excuse to
boost its military spending.

Presidents have to watch what they say. Which means, it's
best to stay on text.

It isn't bad that they have speechwriters, but it is very bad
how they now work with them and use them. John Kennedy
often worked closely with his speechwriters, who held positions of importance in his administration: Ted Sorenson was
his special counsel, Arthur Schlesinger a domestic adviser.
Richard Nixon often worked closely with his speechwriters;
William Safire has written of how he was spun into the president's gravity for weeks at a time when he worked with him on
speeches, and then spun out again.

But Jimmy Carter's speechwriters almost never saw him, and
are frank about how they often had no idea what he was thinking
on any given issue and more often than not had to guess. One of
his writers told Carol Gelderman, author of *All the President's
Words*, "Ghostwriting is an esoteric art, requiring psychological
transference. . . . I can't get into the head of Jimmy Carter
because I've never met Jimmy Carter. The isolation of writers in
the White House—never sitting in on policy discussions, no conference with the president—is like writing in a vacuum."

Ronald Reagan's speechwriters met with him fairly often
before he was shot, but infrequently after. Reagan's aides
had been instructed after the shooting to limit nonessential

demands on the president's time, and they were more than happy to define meetings with speechwriters as nonessential because they viewed the speechwriters as idiots, i.e., serious conservatives. Reagan's aides were always afraid the speechwriters and the president would together cook up something unhelpful like the Evil Empire speech. Which of course was a fine speech in the judgment of conservatives and prisoners of the Gulag, but not so fine in the view of Reagan's top aides, who thought conservative thinking was a form of nonthinking. This is a much-told tale, and I won't go into it except to note that Reagan's speechwriters were saved by one thing, a thing Carter's speechwriters were denied. Too bad, too, for some of them were enormously gifted (Hendrik Hertzberg), or quick and funny (Christopher Mathews). They could have made a great contribution.

What saved Reagan's speechwriters is this: We knew what he thought, why he thought it, and how he'd say it. His views and assumptions were well known and clear; his philosophy had been delineated and explicated in a series of speeches in the sixties and seventies. His style was vividly his own.

Carter's writers dealt with a less clearly drawn man intellectually, philosophically and stylistically. His speeches from the sixties, for instance, were either on local and parochial issues in Georgia, or, when he went national, were a series of yearnings: He wanted a better government for our people but never explained quite how. So I always view the good work of Carter's speechwriters as a triumph against the odds.

(The prissily vengeful James Fallows, Carter's former chief speechwriter, later punished his boss for keeping him out of the loop by turning on Carter during his presidency in a magazine piece. Carter, he said, lacked passion. Many of us thought, No, Carter lacked purposes for passion; he lacked purpose, period. A man who wills himself into the presidency has passion enough, but it may be passion only for himself and his sense of destiny.)

Any speechwriting collaboration, in business or in cultural and political organizations, only works well and produces good work if the principal works closely with the writer. Or, in the case of a president, with his writers and policy people. Otherwise it's no good—for history, for the president, or for the people he serves.

I once wrote about this at great length in a book, and thought it might help change things for the better. It did not. (Actually Clinton has been better than his Republican predecessors on this, but only a bit.) Speechwriters are still left in the void, treated as hacks, and sequestered in the OEOB where, as was famously said of the hostages of Lebanon, they see themselves as mushrooms—covered with manure and left in the dark.

Which is one reason presidential rhetoric in our time has become the thin and uneven thing it is.

But it's always a good idea to be an operational pessimist and an overall optimist, to not expect that a problem will get better today but in the long term must, and therefore will. That future president years down the road who works closely with his speechwriters, includes them in policy discussions and makes them part of the heartbeat of the White House will no doubt benefit greatly in terms of great work created and spoken. It could set a new style, and create a new reigning cliché.

By the way, as most of you probably know, presidential speechwriters are nothing new. Alexander Hamilton wrote some of George Washington's farewell, Lincoln sought out help on his speeches from cabinet secretaries and friends. FDR's great speechwriters not only worked closely with him but drafted much of the literature of the New Deal.

It's not new. It's just badly done now.

Another thought. I sometimes think that modern presidents and businessmen ignore speechwriters for a reason having to do with honesty. They think that speechwriting is by its nature disingenuous—somebody else writes the words!—and they don't want to take too great a part in the dishonesty. They don't want to give too much time to the showbiz of politics. Which, they sometimes think, is what speech giving is.

But speeches aren't showbiz, they are a way to lead. They are a tool of leadership. They are sometimes leadership itself, as the great presidents knew. And if a candidate or president would take a greater role in speechwriting, it would neither seem nor be dishonest.

The answer for a modern president, or candidate, is not detachment but involvement. Honesty can be located, and honored, in the work that follows.

Once I worked on a speech with Oprah Winfrey. I learned something important from that experience.

It is that when you come right down to it, to produce a good speech a collaboration has to have two things. One is a writer who can do the work. The other is a principal who understands that work—who understands its parts, what works and what doesn't, someone who understands the requirements. And meets them in terms of engagement and involvement.

If you are a writer, you might do the best work of your life, but if the person you're writing for isn't really involved, or can't really tell that it is good work, or why and in what way it is, then they'll never understand or appreciate the speech.

And if they don't understand and appreciate it, they'll never absorb it and make it their own. They'll fiddle with it, fret over it, and have their friends take things out and put things in. Which means a committee will have written it. Which means it won't be any good.

So the good writer needs a smart reader who's so involved in the drafting that he or she is a complete coauthor.

Oprah called me with the facts of her speech—when it was, where it was, who would be in the crowd, what time the speech would be given, where she would stand, who would speak before and after her, how long she was expected to talk.

Then she covered the big things, the subject matter and tone. She was to honor a show business titan. He was being given a prestigious award, and she felt he deserved it. She admired his work and told me why. She had worked with him once and described their first meeting. She had learned things from him, sometimes painfully. She told me stories about it. They really tumbled out.

Then she changed focus. After we talk about his work, she said, I want to talk about the nature of work itself. She said, I believe we all have a calling, a reason for doing the work we do, and that we can't do it for small reasons, we have to do it to serve each other, to help people.

As she spoke I took notes, stopping her sometimes to ask her to explain something or to expand on a point. Then I got working, writing from what she told me, using phrase after phrase, story after story, adding connective tissue or rewording an aside.

She called back in a few days. She was thinking about the lives people live in the entertainment industry. They have so much, they have to invent new things to want and have. And yet it never makes them happy, she said. Piling up material things never makes any of us happy. Only good work that is a contribution, that lights the world, gives real satisfaction . . .

That, I thought, would become the end of the speech.

A few days later she called again. She'd remembered something that happened when the man who was to be honored appeared on her show. He had appealed for help in the building of an archive. After the show aired she was driving through a Chicago neighborhood when a man flagged her down. He had a bag of coffee beans in his hand. She stopped and lowered the window. The man said he owned a coffee shop, that he didn't have much but this was what he could give to help the archive. She said, "Everyone wants to give, people want to be part of something larger, they want to help, and that should be honored."

Now that was part of the ending.

When I was done I sent it to her. She called me as soon as she read it. "You got my voice," she said. "How did you do that?"

"You gave it to me," I said. "It was in my notes."

She had spoken to me vividly, colorfully, with the excitement of one intent on what she had to say.

She never stopped working on that speech. It was in her mind for two weeks, she would daydream about it, it was there. If she had anything to do with it, then it was going to be good.

And she had everything to do with it.

So that's what you need from the person you're writing for: someone who knows what it takes and gives it.

That was a great experience. Here was a not-so-great one.

A number of years ago I was contacted by the public relations firm that handles a Fortune 500 company. The company had a new CEO, a dynamic, no-nonsense man with a great reputation not only as a manager but as a shrewd reader of what comes next in his highly competitive field.

The PR firm asked if I would write a speech for him. I was intrigued, and went to see him. He lived up to his billing: intelligent, interesting and quick. A little rough around the edges, but even that was interesting. Most people get smoothed out by the time they're in his position; he'd decided not to. I asked him what he wanted to say in the speech, and he said he wanted to put his oar in on various public policy questions. This wasn't surprising, as business is deeply affected by public policy, but I was impressed as he spoke by the depth and sophistication of his views. I left, decided I'd like to work with him, came back, and we talked some more. He elaborated on his views. He also told some funny stories that had a point, and anecdotes that fit into his general theme.

I thought, what a good person to work with, he knows what he thinks and why he thinks it, knows what he wants to say and understands the elements, he's supplying me with them as I take notes—"And there's another thing I saw in Washington that may fit in here."

I went home and worked for two weeks, trying to organize the material, re-hear and reproduce his voice, cover all the substantive ground he wanted to cover in a way that wasn't too dense and heavy, but . . . light enough to hold and hear. But not so light that it would float away.

When it was done I liked it a lot. I thought, this is an interesting person with a lot to say, people are going to respect his views.

I sent it in to him and heard: nothing. Then I heard through the grapevine that he was disappointed. Why? He didn't think the speech seemed original. He didn't think it had much flash. In fact, he thought it was kind of boring, like something he'd heard before.

I was taken aback, and felt defensive. I'd worked so hard! I'd really tried to capture him and his thoughts, to reveal the quality of his mind.

And then I realized . . . holy mackerel, that's the problem. He *had* heard it all before—he'd told it to me. Of course it didn't seem original—he's old news to him! When I gave him his own sound back he was disappointed—he wanted a new one. He wanted to be reinvented. When I would have thought, and told him, Don't reinvent yourself, you're terrific the way you are.

But we'd never discussed who he wanted to be in the speech. I just assumed he wanted to be him. (And if he'd told me he wanted to be reinvented, I don't know what I could have done for him, for I am not a scientist. Things can be moderated and shaded, but not wholly redone.)

Part of our problem was the magic problem. He may have thought I was going to magically transform him into Reagan or Thatcher or the pope. And not only am I not capable of that, but it would have been silly.

But part of it was unstated expectation. I hadn't asked him what he wanted, and he hadn't told me. If I had, and he had said "I want to be Bill Gates," I could have solved both our problems by saying, "You shouldn't want that and I can't help you."

So I learned something: Ask the question. If they want to be themselves you can work with them, if they want to be someone else you can try to talk them out of it.

But you both should know going in.

Another thing I learned by the way was about writing for people in business. I learned some of it by talking to corporate speechwriters while I worked on the CEO's speech.

One problem that I had anticipated was translation: translating the occasionally strange and arcane lingo of certain businesses, and big business in general, to the common speech of men and women.

Another challenge was that people in business want to break through and make an impression when they speak, but they don't want to be too colorful and draw unwanted attention.

My background was in politics: I'd never met anybody who didn't want attention.

So business speechwriters have to make it good without making it too good, make it sharp without making it so pointed that it winds up being quoted in partial context in an unflattering profile in *Business Week*.

Yet another challenge for corporate speechwriters: Business is not, for most of us, inherently dramatic and fascinating. It's constructive and important, but it doesn't lend itself to the kind of drama political speechwriting can. But businessmen and -women see themselves as leaders—which is fair, they are—and often want to be moving and to rouse the troops as great leaders have throughout history. This is a great challenge, for it is one thing to rouse the troops on D-Day, quite another to try to rouse them to make more and better widgets before the quarter is out.

People at the top in business and people at the top in politics have a lot in common, but there are differences too. What a CEO and a senator have in common is that they are twentieth-century princes. They are used to making other people hop, used to having the car waiting and the helo humming on the pad. And so both can be hard for a writer to work with— they're distracted, too full of movement, sometimes too full of themselves to listen or to engage in back-and-forth.

And there is an interesting difference in emphasis. Politicians want to look good so they can get things done. CEOs want to get things done so they can look good.

Politicians have to burnish their reputations not only to continue being reelected, but to get things accomplished in the Congress or the legislature. A senator thought by the press to be uninteresting, incompetent or dim will be so labeled. His colleagues will notice, and when he comes to them for help in passing a piece of legislation they will ask themselves, Do I want to be associated with a known dunce? They don't. It will hurt their reputations, and they'll get fewer things done. So politicians speak in public always with an eye, first and foremost, to looking good, making an impression, catching attention, earning respect.

CEOs, on the other hand, want to get things done; that's their primary focus. They have to get the stock up, launch the IPO, beat back the lawsuit, challenge the regulation, create the best product. And if they succeed, they will look good. Which brings rewards—more money, pleasure in one's success, more big jobs coming down the pike . . . maybe even in politics. But the key for them is to get things done.

This difference in emphasis grows out of the difference in jobs, and maybe in part a difference in the temperaments of those who go into the one field or the other.

Anyway, for political speechwriters it means that a lot of time has to be devoted to keeping an eye on the press—what will interest them in a speech, what will impress them. For corporate speechwriters it means keeping an undeviating eye on the boss's agenda and making sure the speech advances it. And then, secondarily, they must make sure he looks and sounds good in order to impress people, including the press.

All of this is hard, and it's given me a special sympathy for

corporate speechwriters. They should be given medals for
charging up so many slippery hills.

A final note. I have criticized in this book the aides and
lawyers who fiddle with and wring their hands over speech
drafts. But I want to make a distinction between them and editors. A good editor is hard to find—even harder to find than a
good writer. But when you've got one, you've got gold. An editor can make the difference between success and failure in a
speech.

Mark Helprin is an American novelist of Tolstoyan gifts, the
author of *Winter's Tale* and *A Soldier of the Great War* and writer
of sharp essays for the *Wall Street Journal*. It was Bob Dole's
good fortune that Mark came to him one day in early 1996
and asked to work with him on his speeches. Mark and Dole
worked for weeks on Dole's masterly announcement that he
was leaving the Senate, "just a man" who would run for the
presidency with nothing to fall back on and "nowhere to go
but the White House, or home." (The implication was that
home was Kansas. By 1997, though, home for Dole was still
Washington and a white-shoe law firm. Note to speechwriters:
These things have a way of changing.) The speech was a success not only because Mark is a master but because both men
worked on it intently, faxing it back and forth, learning to
understand each other's way of thinking.

They worked again on Dole's acceptance speech at the
Republican convention in San Diego. But this turned out not
to be so great a success. Helprin had lost none of his talent or
zeal and worked hard, but Dole was distracted—there were so
many other things that demanded attention, and a speech a
month or two weeks away becomes the thing each day that you
put off.

But more important, the convention speech—long, important, fully televised during prime time, delivered in a room full of thousands of delegates—required an experienced editor who fully understood the special requirements and demands of an acceptance speech. But Helprin's editor was one of Dole's aides, a bright and literate man who was hobbled by the fact that he didn't know what he didn't know.

This happens to all of us eventually, and if we're lucky it happens in a low-stakes venture. The aide wasn't lucky.

It takes a certain amount of experience to know what you don't know. If you don't have that experience you'll assume you know pretty much what you have to know. You're not sophisticated enough to see the gaps in your knowledge. You only see them when it's over and things didn't work.

Helprin had written a full draft months before the convention, not a bad way for such a speech to begin because it gives everyone in the process a document they can hold in their hands and focus on. (It also speaks of a passion on the part of the writer—no writer's block there.) Mark had produced a passionate text that had a tone of real political courage. It also had some beautiful passages. But as it was, it would not have worked as a convention speech.

There were some long sections that were austerely declamatory. In some of its subject matter, it was not quite Dole. In its style, it was less Dole-esque than their earlier collaboration. But it was a first draft, and could be fixed.

There were also some problems that arose from the special nature and special demands of an acceptance speech.

Like a presidential inaugural address, an acceptance speech is given before thousands of people who are standing and listening. But at an inaugural people listen silently and respectfully. It is noon on a weekday in winter, and supporters of the new president have come to hear him hoping that in the sound of his voice they will hear: history. The audience is serious and respectful, as befits a group who are about to hear an address that will enter the American archive.

An acceptance speech is different. Convention halls are packed with party regulars and pols, thousands of people in a womp-'em-stomp-'em-go-get-'em mood. The speech takes place at night. The delegates have eaten dinner and had a drink or two. By the time they get to the hall they want to raise Cain and blow horns. They want to act out their support for their candidates for the TV guys who are doing close-ups of their faces. They want the anchors in the anchor booths to say, when the speech is over, "Dole electrified the crowd."

They are wearing elephant hats.

Here's the special challenge:

You cannot ask such a crowd in such circumstances to stand still and listen to extended philosophical discourse. You have to have some fun, you have to let them be bombastic and get their energy out. But at the same time you have to give a serious speech, for you are accepting the nomination of a major political party to become president of the United States. The whole country is watching, and some are seeing you and judging you for the first time. This is your first big opportunity to tell them what you are about. You must address issues of national concern. You must speak in a way that is worthy of the office you desire.

The conflicting demands make it a demanding speech to write. Balance is all. There will be long sections of seriousness, but these passages can be like the movements in a symphony—they are highlighted, underscored, made more beautiful by variation from the movements that precede and follow.

You learn this by doing it. You learn it by writing speeches to be given before thousands of people who want to blow horns. I learned something by being one of the writers who worked on Ronald Reagan's acceptance speech in 1984. We had a beautiful ending. That summer the Olympic torch was being carried from one side of the continent to the other, and every morning on the *Today* show and *Good Morning America* they'd show who was carrying it today—the former Olympic great, the grandma in Nikes, the chief of a local Indian tribe, a kid in a wheelchair. It's always so predictable and yet always so moving, as if you're seeing all of who we are passing by.

We used it in Reagan's peroration. He spoke of the towns the torch went through, evoked the great names of old cities . . . God, it was beautiful.

And a real floparooni.

Because every time Reagan said the name of a town or city our delegates from the states that had been mentioned—all of whom were merry, many of whom were tipsy—would blow their horns and scream. The mood was broken, dispelled. Reagan, who knew what had happened, gave up and started laughing. My friends and I in the stands, we put our heads in our hands and groaned.

This is how you learn what works.

Dole's speech needed the movements. It needed tightening here and expanding there, but mostly it needed the variety of different movements.

It needed, for instance, humor. Dole is a very funny man, so this was a natural, something authentic to him that could be used to great effect. But Mark Helprin is a genius and not a joke writer. And the editor of the speech didn't know humor is necessary any more than he knew movements were necessary.

Humor was needed to let some of the air out of the bal-

loon. The crowd was pumped and ready for action, they had
to be given something to do—laugh, cheer—to settle them
down.

Then, after the humor, you can quiet them with a transi-
tional passage that is neither funny nor demanding but appropriate, interesting. Let them listen. Get more interesting. And
once they've been listening for a while, let them think. Tell
them some of your philosophy, speak of what's serious, say
who you are, how you see the age and the office.

And then give them a joke, a small one, to break the trance
and give them a break. And then give them a better joke or
witticism. And then let them stomp and honk and cheer
again, because that's what they want to do.

They want to think, too. But you have to make it easier for
them by varying the tempo, surprising them.

A small example: Dole at one point said that Bill Clinton
had taken so many Republican ideas that he might as well be
here tonight. It got a nice laugh, and they started blowing
their horns. Dole then got serious—and the crowd got restive.
Because they thought they were going to get a little longer to
act up.

I was there in the hall and thought Dole should have let
them. Here is a stab at one of ten things he could have done:
He could have peered out at the crowd, pointed at some back-
of-the-room delegation, and said, "Is that him?" And then
looked and pointed at another delegation: "Is he over there?
Bill, is that you?"

It would have been a happy, silly break—a television version
of *Where's Waldo?* with a whole country imagining an antic Bill
Clinton running from the California delegation to the Jersey
delegation and delegates chanting, inevitably, "Where's Bill?"

The point is, it might have been fun. And convention

speeches are supposed to be fun. Serious too. But as every natural pol from Lincoln to Reagan knew, fun is part of politics, and not the least honorable part.

Another convention of convention speeches that could have been used to vary the tempo and let out the steam is audience participation, getting the crowd to chant something, yell out an answer. As in, "And will this party move forward, together, and take back the White House?"

Yesssss!

"Will we work together to help the Congress we need win in November?"

Yesssss!

This is a fine old cliché that's just another way to get a crowd quiet by letting them yell. But it also gives the impression of dynamism, as if this party can't be stopped.

Ultimately the speech Mark Helprin had written months before was changed, but not improved. It was marked by a kind of interrupted eloquence. A lovely passage was oddly cut, a lovely section oddly led into; a soaring assertion would be followed by boilerplate.

The boilerplate came from a small group of writers brought in to help out. But the group, brought in at the last minute, could not fully remedy the problems. And inevitably the speech took on a committee feel—death for a serious document. Helprin, who had not been told that other writers had been brought in, and whose calls were no longer being returned—the editor was a busy man—called everyone he'd worked with to thank them and say good-bye, then flew home to his family.

I didn't think Mark was wrong to leave, and certainly he did it with courtesy. But he would have had a good speech if he'd been allowed to rewrite it with an eye to the conventions of convention speeches.

Which he could have done if he'd had an experienced editor, or one who knew what he didn't know and got help.

Note to campaign managers: It isn't only the writers and the candidate who make such things work. The editor is important too.

PRESENTATION

BE YOU

T here are communications professionals who will tell you that there are specific gestures you ought to use when you go on TV or make a speech, particular ways to move your hands or use your voice. I do not think this kind of counsel is helpful, partly because it makes speakers focus on the wrong things (how you look as opposed to what you say) and partly because it ignores a central fact. For fifty years now we have all, in the movies and on TV, seen the small tricks and devices people use in communicating. We've seen the bitten lip, the dramatic raising and lowering of the voice, the chop of the hand on the podium. We've seen it all. Once most of white America had never seen a black preacher give a sermon in a black church; they'd never seen the dramatic raising and then softening of the voice, the repetition of phrases. But now we have. Once, that man was a revelation. Now he is a cliché.

Because we have seen so much, things that we used to see that were original and specific to a person—JFK's mannerisms, say—now seem old and derivative. For we have seen many JFK knockoffs, in politics and elsewhere.

We are experienced watchers. And we've learned a lot.

For instance: If you've never been in a locker room in your

life you would still know how to rouse and inspire a team. You would know because you have seen Pat O'Brien play Knute Rockne, or have seen any number of coaches rouse the boys in any number of TV shows and movies. That may be how Vince Lombardi learned how to do it, and Jimmy Johnson.

We unconsciously imitate. Gary Hart's end came with the Donna Rice story, but his slide began months before when reporters noted his weird adoption of the physical manner-isms of John and Robert Kennedy—the hands going in and out of the jacket pocket, the right hand smoothing and pat-ting the hair on his head. It made him seem inauthentic even for a politician, and so insubstantial.

There's a lot of that going around. Do you find the gentle-man across from you at dinner making a snappy point that seems to require a response? He may be having a Ted Koppel moment. And you just might respond like one of Koppel's guests. "I take your point, but I think what the president clearly intended . . . "

We unconsciously imitate the people we see talking on TV. And it's good to know this, and to try not to do it.

What is the relevance here?

If in a speech you find yourself nonchalantly hanging your hand over the front of the podium and turning your voice into a soft, persuasive growl . . . realize you're having a Bill Clinton moment, and stop. Do you find yourself in public having spasms of homey decency and head-cocked humor? Then you are hav-ing a Reagan moment and must stop, for you are not Reagan.

(I've never seen anyone imitate Newt Gingrich. I suspect it's because he's actually so himself, so Newtonian, so the crea-ture of his brain and not his mannerisms that to imitate him you'd have to imitate how he thinks. Which would, for most of us, be a daunting task.)

For you the speech giver the only answer is to be yourself in your presentation, because although there have already been many Lombardis and O'Briens and Rathers and Brokaws and Jesse Jacksons, you are the only you. So you might as well be you, and have a good time.

If you find you have a particular nondistracting habit when you speak (and I do mean nondistracting)—if you have a tendency when you make a point to nod your head in a certain way, or a habit of joining your hands in a little clap when driving home a point—keep it. Use it. Don't let your spouse tell you not to do it because it seems so different. Do it for that reason.

At least it will be authentic. And authenticity in the age of media isn't just half the battle, it's a real achievement, a triumph almost.

I'm thinking at the moment of Steve Forbes. In interviews he has a way of blinking now and then as if in surprise. No one else in national politics does this. He only does it because he does it, and no one's told him not to. I hope no one does, and if they do I hope he doesn't listen, because he is the only candidate out there right now who seems, to me at least, to be just himself. Seeing him is a kind of relief.

By the way, on the difference between distracting and nondistracting habits: Something is distracting if it is so unusual or unpleasant that it starts to bug the audience, which starts to whisper, "I hate the way he keeps scratching his head, does he have fleas?" instead of "He's right about the Serbs." How can you tell if a habit is distracting? Your friends in the audience will tell you after the speech. If they ask, pleasantly, if you have a scalp condition, realize you have been distracting them.

Somewhat off the point but what the heck:

These days, when sitting in restaurants or diners and seeing
people sit up straight and speak to each other and tell stories
and offer opinions, I have taken to wondering how people
moved their faces before everyone learned How People Move
Their Faces. Was it different seventy-five years ago, before
movies and television taught us all how people look when they
say something? How they move their faces when they say "I
love you" or "This must stop"? Were people less aware of looking "the right way"? Were they less self-conscious?

This has led me to wonder what it was like before mirrors,
before people got to stand in front of a mirror and see how
they look when they're worried, or how their face moves when
they imitate the guy in the hut next door when he's angry.

My thought—actually, I think it is my hope—is that seventy-
five and five hundred years ago people were more highly indi-
vidualistic in their expressions, more dramatic, more full of
grimaces and heartbreaking smiles. Maybe sometimes they
looked like people in hospitals for the mentally ill in the old
days, the predrug days, for the insane are less self-conscious
than others.

People, before movies and TV and mirrors, must have
looked more often like how they felt.

This is another way the age of communication has made
our ability to communicate with each other less clear and colorful. We're all pretty much smoothed out now, like patients in
modern hospitals who are on medication.

Don't Forget to Say Thanks

T he old cliché is that you should always, at the top of a speech, thank the people who invited you and the person who introduced you. The new cliché is that you should never, at the top of a speech, thank the people who invited you and the person who introduced you. The thinking here is that it's boring and predictable and you lose the audience.

But I don't think so. It's not boring to be polite, it's merely expected. And saying thanks at the top has a practical purpose. While you're doing it the audience gets a chance to daydream and free-associate: "Oh, I like his glasses." "That's a nice suit." "He looks like Jimmy—oh, I gotta call him." This isn't bad. They're going to daydream at some point anyway, and it might as well be before you get to the heart of your remarks.

You don't have to go on too long, but don't be perfunctory—"Thanks, Helen, nice introduction. And thanks to the Young Presidents' Organization. My subject tonight is the change that has swept the fast-food industry." Say your thanks in the manner, or with the tone, of someone who's been invited to a party, is happy to be there and just walked in the door to shake the host's hand. You say thanks, that you really looked forward to it; you offer a compliment or some warm words.

That's all that's needed.

Sometimes introducers get carried away, and their introductions demand a response.

After her column and television appearances made her a hot item on the speech circuit, Erma Bombeck wrote an essay about what she thinks about when she hears people introduce her.

She wrote, "Sometimes the accolades are so glowing that I don't even recognize myself. I figure Mother Teresa just flew in to give the invocation. Other times I feel like bolting while I'm still ahead. But most of the time I feel as though the only decent thing I can do to justify such a tribute is to die. Occasionally I allow myself to look at the audience and try to figure out if they believe any of it."

Then she said the worst part about her bio is that it's so flattering because she wrote it.

After I read this I did what any self-respecting speechwriter eager to continue the traditions of her craft would do. I stole it. The next time I made a speech I thanked Joe or Sue for the introduction, noted that it was almost embarrassingly flattering and said as an aside that that might be because I wrote it. It surprised people, and made us all laugh.

There are some ol' reliables that I've always liked, responses to introductions that certain speakers have used. Lyndon Johnson used to say, "That was the kind of very generous introduction that my father would have appreciated, and my mother would have believed." Walter Mondale would say, feelingly, "I don't deserve those kind words. But then I have arthritis and I don't deserve that either." After a flat or too-

perfunctory introduction Mondale would look at the intro-
ducer, and then at the audience, and deadpan, "Of all the
introductions I've ever received, that was the most recent."

Once I saw the comedian Howie Mandel respond to being
introduced. As I remember it, he had returned to the college
he had years before attended and was to address the student
body. The speech was taped and later carried on HBO.

Mandel was obviously excited and bounded onto the stage
with a big smile. He grabbed the lectern, one of those big
brown wooden things, looked out and blurted, "If I'd known
there was going to be a podium, I wouldn't have worn pants!"
It was weirdly delightful and made everyone laugh. But it
probably wouldn't work for Walter Mondale.

Erma Bombeck, by the way, suggested a new wrinkle in
introductions to make them more palatable for the audience.

She said we ought to list not the speaker's successes, but his
failures. In her case, the introduction could be, "Tonight's
speaker needs an introduction or I wouldn't be standing here
in a rented tuxedo and shoes the wrong width. Born average,
our guest tonight never rose above it. At Ohio University, her
guidance counselor advised her to go into anything but journalism. At age seventeen, when Queen Elizabeth had her own
country, she was writing a column for three dollars a week for
an Ohio weekly. . . ."

She recounted how her first comedy album "raced to obliv-
ion," that she has written numerous plays "no one ever heard
of because they never made it to the stage," that she never
won a Pulitzer and was never interviewed by Barbara Walters.

Bombeck said such an introduction would be a good idea
because failing is what most of us do. "We do that a lot more
than we succeed. Sometimes an audience figures we've led
such charmed lives." But why would a big crowd of people

stick around to hear a speech from a failure? "Because despite all the disappointments and the failures, she's still managed to go on breathing and put them aside . . . and to an audience, that's something worth listening to."

I'll bet the next speech Erma Bombeck made after that column came out, she got that for an introduction. And I'll bet it was funny. But—of course—this approach would work only if the person you're introducing is one of unarguable achievement and natural confidence, like Erma Bombeck.

Graciousness springs from a generosity of spirit. It is good. And it can light a speech in subtle ways.

Gracious people naturally try to make those around them comfortable. They have, and show, appreciation and respect for those around them. One way to make the people on the dais with you comfortable, or to make those who invited you to speak comfortable, is to acknowledge them and, if you can, compliment them on some aspect of their work. "Governor X has asked me to speak about how to improve the quality of life in the states of the Southwest. But my first thought was probably similar to yours: Maybe he should be speaking. In his time in office this state has experienced a historic number of new businesses, a record number of housing starts, and the biggest property tax cut of any state in the union. The legislature deserves credit, but I think the governor deserves the lion's share because he led the way, spoke for progress and drafted the bills. He'll be speaking later, and like most of you I'll be staying to hear him. But every state that's enjoying a comeback can take steps to see that the comeback is institutionalized—that it doesn't disappear under the next legislature or the one after that. And that is what I'm going to speak about."

What you say must not only be true, it must be understood

to be true by the audience. If the governor or Kiwanis president or CEO has a famously irascible temperament it won't do to claim otherwise—"I think the boom is connected to the governor's personal charm, his merriness and warmth."

Fabricate or exaggerate and your audience will lose faith in you and dismiss what follows.

If there really is nothing nice to say, say nothing. But then I think you should ask yourself: Why am I here? Maybe you shouldn't be.

Or maybe you're not seeing some real virtues. Sometimes you have to look.

TOASTS AND TRIBUTES

T oasts are a great torment but shouldn't be. Giving one should be as easy as telling a friend why you love him. The challenge, of course, is that you're doing it in front of people and trying not to stutter or drop your glass. You're also trying to be clever. Don't try too hard; there's a great myth that you have to be a great wit at these things, but you don't. It would be good to be original, unique even, but in our world you do this not with cleverness but with sincerity.

All good toasts are sincere. You don't have to be funny. Funny is the bow on the gift, not the gift. You don't have to be profound. But what you say must be true or sound true, and it will probably only be the latter if it is the former.

If you have been asked to toast someone it's because you are thought to have great affection for him or her. If you do, agree to give the toast. (If you don't, don't. A lukewarm tribute is like lukewarm champagne; it tastes flat and is only remembered because it wasn't good.) Then show your affection by explaining why you feel it.

A toast should probably go five or six minutes or less. It can be more depending on the circumstances and your ability.

The most famous toast of our day is probably the one Hugh

Grant gave before the friends and relatives of the bride and groom at the wedding lunch in *Four Weddings and a Funeral*. I use it as an example of the kind of toast you must never give:

> Ladies and gentlemen, I'm sorry to drag you from your delicious desserts. There are just one or two things I feel I should say as best man. This is only the second time I've been a best man. I hope I did the job all right that time. The couple in question are at least still talking to me. Unfortunately they're not actually still talking to each other. The divorce came through a couple of months ago. But I'm sure it had absolutely nothing to do with me. Apparently Paula knew that Pierce had slept with her younger sister before I mentioned it in the speech. The fact that he'd slept with her mother came as a surprise, but I think that was incidental to the nightmare of recrimination and violence that became their two-day marriage. Anyway, enough of that. My job today is to talk about Angus. And there are no skeletons in his cupboard. Or so I thought. I'll come on to that in a minute. I would just like to say this: I am, as ever, in bewildered awe of anyone who makes this kind of commitment that Angus and Laura have made today. I know I couldn't do it, and I think it's wonderful they can. So anyway, back to Angus and those sheep. Ladies and gentlemen, if you would raise your glasses: the adorable couple."

Now there are five reasons you should never give a toast like this, and you know all of them. Suffice it to say this was good screenwriting and bad toast giving. Oh, here's a sixth reason not to give one like it: Bad taste is a virus that gains strength as it spreads. People want to imitate it and outdo it. This even happened in the movie. After the laughter of Hugh Grant's toast had died away another best man at another wed-

ding stood to speak. Having witnessed the success of Grant's
earlier effort, he tried to ape it: "When Bernard told me he
was getting engaged to Lydia I congratulated him because all
his other girlfriends had been such complete dogs. Although
may I say how delighted we are to have so many of them here
this evening. I'm particularly delighted to see Camilla, who
many of you will probably remember as the first person
Bernard asked to marry him. If I remember rightly, she told
him to sod off. And lucky for Lydia, he did."

This was followed by silence, and another guest's comment
that he seemed to be stuck in the wedding from hell. Anyway,
you can lose an empire doing things like this, so don't.

Here's a good recent toast given by the businessman Pete
Peterson, Richard Nixon's former secretary of Commerce, to
the writer Liz Smith at a 1996 birthday party in her honor in
New York. It was a highly sophisticated audience of glittering
adults, and Peterson's tribute reflected this. What distinguishes his toast is not only that it was sincere, but that highest
of compliments: It was thought through.

> You all know how it goes at parties like this when you are asked
> to make a toast. . . . You mean to stand up and tell the guest of
> honor how much you love her, and then you can't resist the
> temptation to roast the hell out of her.
>
> But tonight I'm actually going to make some serious points
> about our girl here. We do all know Liz, and we all love her. But
> it occurred to me in the past few years that when the social histo-
> rians of the future look back at our day, the cleverest of them
> will see something interesting. They will see that the journalist
> Liz Smith broke the rules, broke the mold, and created a new
> art form: compassionate gossip.

You know, I've collected oxymorons since my Washington days, beginning with "powerful secretary of Commerce." And until Liz came along, the words "classy gossip columnist" were an oxymoron.

Liz, from the time she started her *Daily News* column many years ago, has been the most startling and striking combination of kindhearted and insightful. Or maybe I should say she's been "warmly astringent." Or "sweet-naturedly unsentimental." But whatever you call it, it's unusual to say the least.

Walter Winchell sometimes tried to be warm, and when he did he was cloying. Dorothy Kilgallen was sometimes insightful, but no one ever accused her of sweetness. I mention Winchell and Kilgallen because they were pioneer columnists, very big in their day, as Liz is, but they didn't have what Liz has. They didn't have her live-and-let-live sensibility. They kind of dug lower down in the gossip bin for their items.

Liz very famously doesn't do gossip on certain things, on someone running around on his wife or someone running around on her husband—unless they call and tell her, of course.

Which they sometimes do. Because they know she'll listen with compassion. And it's a compassion and capacity for sympathy that are so real, so genuine, that they don't seem to notice that she's taking notes.

Others in the gossip business always used a shovel, but Liz's specialty has always been the scoop. And like the great journalist she is, she has broken an extraordinary number of stories and had loads of exclusives.

It was Liz who broke the story of JFK Jr.'s impending marriage. She broke it in 1991 and the bride was Darryl Hannah, but still. . . .

So respected is she among celebrities, Madonna actually phoned Liz to reveal her pregnancy—and that was during the conception.

And Liz has never been reluctant to give advice. She's even close to royalty. She gave a lot of counsel to Princess Diana, though I'm not sure they're still speaking. Early in the royal marriage, Liz told her, "I just saw a picture of Camilla Parker Bowles and believe me, you have nothing to worry about."

Sorry, Liz, I couldn't resist a little roast.

But seriously, it was the huge success of Liz's column a quarter century ago that led to the explosion of gossip as an industry in America. Before her a lot of it was a small and decorous world of celebrities in Stork Clubs, their comings and goings chronicled in boldfaced items. But after Liz came along and added her sensibility to that whole world, to the glamour culture, hundreds of imitators sprang up, in the seventies and eighties and nineties, in newspapers and magazines. And there was E entertainment channel and *Entertainment Tonight* and *Entertainment Weekly* and the stunning popularity of the *National Enquirer* and the *Star.* . . .

A whole industry was created by our Miss Smith. And you know, Liz, since a lot of the people here tonight are celebrities, many of us would just like to punch you in the nose for that.

But the social historians will attest that it all started in the early 1970s, with the textured, interesting, column-length mini-essays of our fair-haired girl from Texas. . . .

She has been a big star for twenty-five years now, but she is probably the humblest person in this room—because she still knows she's lucky. Many of us forget our own luck, but she still knows. That she's lucky to be born with her gifts, to use them at full capacity, lucky to live in this time, lucky to be here.

And as lucky as she is we're luckier, because she's our friend. . . . She is a party, a pal, and living proof that generosity is great for the complexion. She is the first one to show up with champagne when you're in the pink, and the first to show up with a double vodka when you're blue. . . .

So a toast to Liz, to our best boldfaced girl, our really stupen-
dously loving and well-loved friend.

It was a little long for a toast, but it didn't seem long. And
Liz said she would never forget it. Which was the point: Peterson told me he wanted to give her a gift she could keep for a
long time.

TRIBUTES

The head of Prudential Insurance is leaving, you've been a
close friend and board member for twenty years and they ask
you to speak at the company-wide meeting where they'll say
good-bye. The woman who runs the science department at the
local high school is leaving to fulfill her lifelong dream to live
in a cottage in the west of Ireland, and you have been asked to
speak at the lunch. The campaign is over, and you want to
thank everyone who worked for you. The library of a former
U.S. president is holding a fund raiser, and they've asked you,
the current president, to speak.

You're going to give a tribute, try to sum up the contribution, and the meaning of that contribution, of the person or
persons being honored. In a way it's like a toast, but it's longer.

Again, sincerity is the key. You don't have to be Pericles. You
have to speak about why the departure of the person being honored is a loss, and why their presence was or is a benefit.

Sometimes you just want to capture a moment in time. The
irritatingly naive yet nonetheless riveting documentary *The
War Room,* about the workers and volunteers of the Little Rock
office of the 1992 Clinton campaign, received kudos from crit-
ics, but I don't remember many of them mentioning what

seemed to me the most moving moment in the film. It was the speech given by Clinton campaign manager James Carville the night before the voting. He was surrounded by happy, pumped young people who had just worked their first big campaign. Now they were on the verge of what had seemed only months before an impossible victory. They crammed into what looked like a big storage room to listen to the man who had been their leader and friend.

"There's a simple doctrine," said Carville.

Outside of a person's love, the most sacred thing that they can give is their labor. And somehow along the way we tend to forget that.

And labor is a very precious thing that you have. And any time you can combine labor with love, you've made a merger.

And I think we're gonna win tomorrow. And I think the governor is gonna fulfill his promise and change America. And I think that many of you are gonna go on and help him.

I'm a political professional. That's what I do for a living, and I'm proud of it. And we changed the way campaigns are run. Used to be there was a hierarchy—put you on one floor, you didn't go to another floor. If you were someone in an organizational chart, there was no room for you there. Everybody was compartmentalized.

And you people showed that you could be trusted. Everybody in this room, everybody.

And people are gonna tell you you're lucky. You're not. Ben Hogan said, "Golf is a game of luck, the more I practice the luckier I get." The harder you work, the luckier you are.

I was thirty-three years old before I ever went to Washington or New York, forty-two before I won my first campaign. And I'm happy for all of you. You've been part of something special in my life. And I'll never forget what y'all done. Thank you.

It was moving. Carville choked up during the speech, the young workers who had just spent a year of their lives visiting history choked up. Heck, when I saw it, I choked up. Carville is known for spin and bluster, but this speech was genuine and true, and everyone who heard it could tell. You can read it and think, it doesn't quite scan. But when you heard it, it scanned. That can happen when you mean it.

When President Reagan was asked one day in 1984 to speak at a fund-raiser at Teddy Kennedy's house for the JFK Library, he quickly accepted, thereby becoming the first president since Kennedy's death not to defensively dodge the JFK mystique but to confidently embrace it.

Reagan was always eager to reach out to Democrats. In the JFK tribute he implicitly complimented them by honoring their great modern hero:

> It always seemed to me that he was a man of the most interesting contradictions, very American contradictions. We know from his many friends and colleagues, we know in part from the testimony available at the library, that he was both self-deprecating and proud, ironic and easily moved, highly literate yet utterly at home with the common speech of the working man. He was a writer who could expound with ease on the moral forces that shaped John Calhoun's political philosophy; on the other hand, he betrayed a most delicate and refined appreciation for Boston's political wards and the characters who inhabited them. He could cuss a blue streak—but then, he'd been a sailor.
>
> He loved history and approached it as both romantic and realist. He could quote Stephen Vincent Benet on General Lee's army: "The aide-de-camp knew certain lines of Greek / And other things quite fitting for peace but not so suitable for war."

And he could sum up a current "statesman" with an earthy epithet that would leave his audience weak with laughter. One sensed that he loved mankind as it was, in spite of itself, and that he had little patience with those who would perfect what was really not meant to be perfect.

As a leader, as a president, he seemed to have a good, hard, unillusioned understanding of man and his political choices. He had written a book as a very young man about why the world slept as Hitler marched on; and he understood the tensions between good and evil in the history of man—understood, indeed, that much of the history of man can be seen in the constant working out of that tension. . . .

He was a patriot who summoned patriotism from the heart of a sated country. It is a matter of pride to me that so many young men and women who were inspired by his bracing vision and moved by his call to "Ask not" serve now in the White House, doing the business of government.

Which is not to say I supported John Kennedy when he ran for president, because I didn't. I was for the other fellow. But you know, it's true: When the battle's over and the ground is cooled, well, it's then that you see the opposing general's valor.

He would have understood. He was fiercely, happily partisan, and his political fights were tough—no quarter asked and none given. But he gave as good as he got, and you could see that he loved the battle.

Everything we saw him do seemed to show a huge enjoyment of life; he seemed to grasp from the beginning that life is one fast-moving train, and you have to jump aboard and hold on to your hat and relish the sweep of the wind as it rushes by. You have to enjoy the journey, it's ungrateful not to. I think that's how his country remembers him, in his joy.

And when he died, when that comet disappeared over the

continent, a whole nation grieved and would not forget. A tailor in New York put up a sign—"CLOSED DUE TO A DEATH IN THE FAMILY." The sadness was not confined to us. "They cried the rain down that night," said a journalist in Europe. They put his picture up in huts in Brazil and tents in the Congo, in offices in Dublin and Danzig. That was one of the things he did for his country, for when they honored him they were honoring someone essentially, quintessentially, completely American. . . .

Many men are great, but few capture the imagination and the spirit of the times. The ones who do are unforgettable. Four administrations have passed since John Kennedy's death, five presidents have occupied the Oval Office, and I feel sure that each of them thought of John Kennedy now and then, and his thousand days in the White House.

And sometimes I want to say to those who are still in school, and who sometimes think that history is a dry thing that lives in a book: Nothing is ever lost in that house; some music plays on.

I have been told that late at night when the clouds are still and the moon is high you can just about hear the sound of certain memories brushing by. You can almost hear, if you listen close, the whir of a wheelchair rolling by and the sound of a voice calling out, "And another thing, Eleanor!" Turn down a hall and you hear the brisk strut of a fellow saying, "Bully! Absolutely ripping!" Walk softly now and you're drawn to the soft notes of a piano and a brilliant gathering in the East Room, where a crowd surrounds a bright young president who is full of hope and laughter.

I don't know if this is true, but it's a story I've been told. And it's not a bad one, because it reminds us that history is a living thing that never dies—history is not only made by people, it is people. And so history, as young John Kennedy demonstrated, is as heroic as you want it to be, as heroic as you are.

Really, generosity is at the heart of any good tribute. You focus on a person or persons and try to see them with your kindest, most generous eyes. We are all of us flawed, but we all have brilliant gifts. The writer of a good tribute focuses on those gifts, explains them and illustrates them.

EULOGIES

Eulogies are like toasts and tributes in that they are an appreciation of a human being. The difference, of course, is that the human being honored is gone, and you are speaking not to him but to his grieving and sorrowful relatives and friends. Another difference is that you, too, are grieving; you were close to the departed, which is why you have been asked to speak.

A eulogy is not the proper place to show your ambivalence about how the recently departed made his money or treated his ma. It is the place to consider and highlight his obvious virtues—humor, warmth, steadfastness, insouciance, courage— and illustrate them if you can through anecdotes or pictures. "The first time I met him he was sitting under a tree with his ankles crossed, reading a book of poetry. It was finals week at Penn State, but unlike the rest of us he was the picture of ease. I found in forty years of knowing him that that first sight revealed his essential style—an easiness about life, a comfortableness with it, a sense that you shouldn't sweat the small stuff, and that most of it is small stuff. . . ."

A gentle humor is not inappropriate, and can lift people out of the moment; laughter leavens sorrow. But the comedy territory is obviously limited; as the Irish might say, you'll be wanting to save the belly laughs for the burial.

When the veteran *Time* magazine correspondent Richard

Clurman died of a heart attack his friend the publisher Harry Evans was one of the people asked to speak at the funeral. Harry bounded to the podium, looked at the audience with authority and tapped the microphone three times. "What about Dick Clurman?" he said. The overflow crowd laughed and applauded. That was how Dick had announced the topic of the evening at his dinner parties, tapping his wine glass and growling, "What about ... " whatever, whomever: Quemoy and Matsu, Jimmy Carter, Madonna. Dick always wanted to know what's up, what's happening, who's breaking through, who's down and out, what's on the way. Harry caught all that with humor in a eulogy about Dick's lovely, hungry mind.

It is a eulogy that is the most famous speech of the 1990s, the breathtaking address of Earl Spencer at the funeral of his sister Diana, the Princess of Wales. I think that so far it is the only great speech of the 1990s, because in it he said serious things in an unforgettable way—and the whole world was watching.

I write one week after the speech was given and it is still, as it was one minute after it was given, being called controversial. It probably will always be called controversial, because most of those who are paid to give opinions for a living—columnists, journalists, editorial writers, me—will always so label it. But I think I correctly perceive that the speech is a settled matter, and not a matter of controversy, for those who are called "the people"—i.e., those who simply live, watch, conclude, who are not paid to have opinions for a living—have given the speech their approval.

The opinion elite call the speech angry, but I think it was more pointed and uncompromising than angry. They say he lashed out, but I think he skewered. They say he made his nephews, the princes William and Harry, uncomfortable, but the princes are reported by those on the scene to have been the only members of the royal family who applauded.

The speech was not a charitable and kindly document, and it can certainly be argued that it betrayed insufficient compassion for the Queen, who after all braved the blitz as a child with her courageous parents, and who learned from them that emotions are not all, are indeed not much, that a stern sense of duty and a self-denying determination are the virtues that must be cultivated by the truly mature person and the truly responsible royal. She is of another time, and not a worse one. Nor was the speech kind to the much-abused Prince Charles, who was, as a friend of his put it, "pole-axed" by the cruel and brutal death of the mother of his children.

But for all that, how would you like to have the kind of brother who stood up for you so, who stood alone to speak truth to power in front of a few billion people? He spoke what he felt and thought was the unshined truth, and he seemed to be doing it without care for consequences, always an interesting thing to see, and a moving and unusual one, too.

Spencer did not try to be eloquent, he didn't pull out the emotional stops, he did not try to make his listeners cry. He tried instead to make them think about the nature of "the irreplaceable Diana." He clearly decided his remarks had a job— to capture her, to consider the meaning of her life and death, and to throw down the gauntlet to those whom he saw as primarily responsible for much of her pain, the press and the royal family.

He attempted to tell the truth as he saw it, clearly. But when you tell the truth clearly, without flourish, directly—and it is a truth worth hearing—chances are you will be very eloquent indeed.

And because he spoke at a moment of such high drama,

and with the whole world watching, and because his words strikingly met the speech's objectives, Earl Spencer gave, on September 6, 1997, what is so far the one great and unforgettable speech of the 1990s.

Here is the text in full. I'm going to do a little commentary on it when I think something can be pointed out or highlighted, but you might jump the commentary and stick with the text to get its full force, especially if you haven't read it or heard it in a while.

> I stand before you today, the representative of a family in grief, in a country in mourning, before a world in shock.

Right away you know you are in good rhetorical hands, with the balance of phrasing and the building up from the small (family) to the larger (country) to the largest (world). The fact that it is concise—not a word is wasted—signals the seriousness to come.

> We are all united, not only in our desire to pay our respects to Diana, but rather in our need to do so, because such was her extraordinary appeal that the tens of millions of people taking part in this service all over the world via television and radio, who never actually met her, feel that they too lost someone close to them in the early hours of Sunday morning.

That sentence is difficult to say, but he said it. Remember where I said don't write undeliverable sentences? There are exceptions.

> It is a more remarkable tribute to Diana then I can ever hope to offer to her today.

Graceful: "You at home watching have spoken with your
passionate concern more than I can with my poor words."

Diana was the very essence of compassion, of duty, of style, of beauty.
All over the world she was the symbol of selfless humanity, a stan-
dard-bearer for the rights of the truly downtrodden, a very British
girl who transcended nationality. Someone with a natural nobility
who was classless and who proved in the last year that she needed no
royal title to continue to generate her particular brand of magic.

To compliment his sister in a way that criticized her tor-
mentors was deft indeed.

Now the speech changes from one directed at the listeners to
one directed at his sister. I suspect he changed direction in order
to be able to take the gloves off—a broad sally to the abbey would
not be as effective as personal words to a beloved sister.

Today is our chance to say thank you for the way you brightened
our lives, even though God granted you but half a life. We will
all feel cheated always that you were taken from us so young,
and yet we must learn to be grateful that you came at all.

Only now that you are gone do we truly appreciate what we
are without, and we want you to know that life without you is
very, very difficult.

This is the kind of plainness of speech that only people who
are telling the truth can use. They don't need big phrases,
"Oh Diana, we shall never recover."

We have all despaired for our loss over the past week, and only
the strength of the message you gave us through your years of
giving has afforded us the strength to move forward.

There is a temptation to rush to canonize your memory. There is no need to do so. You stand tall enough as a human being of unique qualities, and do not need to be seen as a saint.

Indeed, to sanctify your memory would be to miss out on the very core of your being—your wonderfully mischievous sense of humor, with a laugh that bent you double, your joy for life transmitted wherever you took your smile, and the sparkle in those unforgettable eyes, your boundless energy which you could barely contain.

I thought "with a laugh that bent you double" beautiful.

But your greatest gift was your intuition, and it was a gift you used wisely. This is what underpinned all your other wonderful attributes.

And if we look to analyze what it was about you that had such a wide appeal, we find it in your instinctive feel for what was really important in all our lives.

Without your God-given sensitivity, we would be immersed in greater ignorance at the anguish of AIDS and HIV sufferers, the plight of the homeless, the isolation of lepers, the random destruction of land mines.

Diana explained to me once that it was her innermost feelings of suffering that made it possible for her to connect with her constituency of the rejected.

And here we come to another truth about her. For all the status, the glamour, the applause, Diana remained throughout a very insecure person at heart, almost childlike in her desire to do good for others so she could release herself from deep feelings of unworthiness, of which her eating disorders were merely a symptom.

I found this a fascinating section. The beginning—"And here we come to another truth . . . "—was so old-English, so like a Cambridge professor: "And here Dickens reveals what he is really up to." But what followed—"very insecure," "eating disorders"—was so modern as to be almost jarring. But it did not jar, it made you lean in with interest.

The world sensed this part of her character and cherished her vulnerability.

The last time I saw Diana was on July first, her birthday, in London, when, typically, she was not taking time to celebrate her special day with friends but was guest of honor at a fund-raising charity evening. She sparkled, of course.

But I would rather cherish the days I spent with her in March when she came to visit me and my children at our home in South Africa. I am proud of the fact that, apart from when she was on public display meeting President Mandela, we managed to contrive to stop the ever-present paparazzi from getting a single picture of her. That meant a lot to her.

These are days I will always treasure. It was as if we were transported back to our childhood, when we spent such an enormous amount of time together as the two youngest in the family.

Fundamentally she hadn't changed at all from the big sister who mothered me as a baby, fought with me at school, who endured those long journeys between our parents' homes with me at weekends.

I found this sentence the most wincingly sad in the speech. The last reference was to visitation, the grueling fact of life of all children of divorced parents. In the days after the speech there were those who said this reference was cruel to his and

Diana's mother, who was among the mourners in the Abbey. This may well be true. But I also think it's true that the children of divorce rarely get to say what divorce is; and it is not terrible for society that the earl here used his speech to tell the world some of how children experience it.

It is a tribute to her level-headedness and strength that despite the most bizarre life imaginable after her childhood, she remained intact, true to herself.

There is no doubt she was looking for a new direction in her life at this time.

She talked endlessly of getting away from England, mainly because of the treatment that she received at the hands of the newspapers. I don't think she ever understood why her genuinely good intentions were sneered at by the media, why there appeared to be a permanent quest on their behalf to bring her down.

It is baffling. My own and only explanation is that genuine goodness is threatening to those at the opposite end of the moral spectrum.

That was a stiletto at the heart of hypocrisy. It is also why the speech will always be called controversial: The media understood they were being insulted.

It is a point to remember that of all the ironies about Diana, perhaps the greatest was this: A girl given the name of the ancient goddess of hunting was, in the end, the most hunted person of the modern age.

Painful again. You could see her, in your mind's eye, fleeing like a big-eyed doe the riflelike lenses of the paparazzi.

She would want us today to pledge ourselves to protecting her beloved boys, William and Harry, from a similar fate, and I do this here, Diana, on your behalf.

As he made this pledge he looked out and addressed his sister's casket.

We will not allow them to suffer the anguish that used regularly to drive you to tearful despair. And beyond that, on behalf of your mother and sisters, I pledge that we, your blood family, will do all we can to continue the imaginative and loving way in which you were steering these two exceptional young men, so that their souls are not simply immersed by duty and tradition but can sing openly, as you planned.

We fully respect the heritage into which they have both been born, and will always respect and encourage them in their royal role.

"Your blood family" was stinging toward the Windsors. But "the heritage" and "the royal role" showed respect for them and their efforts.

But we, like you, recognize the need for them to experience as many different aspects of life as possible to arm them spiritually and emotionally for the years ahead. I know you would have expected nothing less from us.

Having said his peace to the Windsors and the world, he turned from his dead sister to address her sons:

William and Harry, we all care desperately for you today. We are all chewed up with sadness at the loss of a woman who wasn't even our mother. How great your suffering is we cannot even imagine.

I would like to end by thanking God for the small mercies he has shown us at this dreadful time, for taking Diana at her most beautiful and radiant and when she had joy in her private life.

Above all, we give thanks for the life of a woman I'm so proud to be able to call my sister—the unique, the complex, the extraordinary and irreplaceable Diana, whose beauty, both internal and external, will never be extinguished from our minds.

As eloquent as all of this was, it was matched by the simple picture, moments later, of the Earl Spencer, seated by himself in the abbey, looking down at the floor in grief.

He had delivered a wonderful tribute to his sister, and an unforgettable tribute for many millions of watchers and listeners who had hoped that someone would put into words their grief. He did. You can't do better than he did.

The great challenge in a eulogy is to try to comfort the grieving when you can't really remove much of their suffering. But still you must try. I think clarity comforts: Capturing well the spirit of the person who died is a kind of compliment that consoles. Expressing the grief of the people who cannot speak offers consolation, too. People always, no matter what the circumstance, like to be able to say, "That's exactly how I feel," or "That's what I was thinking this morning."

Sometimes it's harder than others, no matter who you are.

In December 1985, an Army transport plane carrying 248 soldiers of the 101st Airborne, the Screaming Eagles, crashed on takeoff in Gander, Newfoundland. They were returning from peacekeeping duty in the Mideast. When they left Cairo they were singing raucous carols; they were coming home for Christmas. All aboard perished.

It was the kind of tragedy that leaves people wordless, the kind that for a long time you cannot absorb. President Reagan, their commander in chief, was personally shaken. Now he would speak in a hangar in Kentucky to the families and friends who had been left behind. Reagan knew he had to try to comfort, but he wondered, as all givers of eulogies wonder, how? I worked with him on his remarks, and knew only that Reagan was thinking what America was thinking: God, all those young men—and their families getting the news at Christmastime. I also knew that when an American president comes and tells you your son's life had meaning it will not lessen your grief, but it offers an accompaniment to it, something you can put next to your sadness and think about, in time. Another thought: I had seen over the years that there are two terrible things that consciously or unconsciously go through people's minds under these circumstances. One is that the true horror of death for survivors is not that we cannot go on without the one who died, but that we can. The extra grief of that going on, the fact that the rug of life has been pulled from under you and yet the next morning the birds sing, the paper hits the door, the lady from Visa calls to say you're overdue . . . this is the horror of death, the crudity with which it changes almost nothing. When, like Auden, you want the world to stop, the police to wear black gloves, the planes to write your sadness in the sky. And the second thing is the particular feeling you have when young people die—the sense of "How could this be, what could this mean?" The mystery of it, a life interrupted when it hadn't had time to unspool, unfurl, reveals itself and its meaning. No one gets to prepare for the deaths of young people who go down in a plane or skid off a highway. You beat yourself because you didn't love them enough, which is always true, because no one is loved enough.

But Reagan believed in God. He believed there was a purpose in all things, a hidden coherence. And so, when he spoke, he talked of the tragedy, of the peacekeeping mission and its purpose. And then he talked to the parents, who sat before him in muffled rows.

Tragedy is nothing new to mankind, but somehow it's always a surprise, never loses its power to astonish. Those of us who did not lose a brother or son or daughter or friends are shaken nonetheless. . . . We cannot fully share the depth of your sadness, but we pray that the special power of this season will make its way into your sad hearts and remind you of some old joys.

Remind you of the joy it was to know these fine young men and women, the joy it was to witness the things they said and the jokes they played, the kindnesses they did, and how they laughed.

You were part of that, you who mourn: You were part of them. And just as you think today of the joy they gave you, think for a moment of the joy you gave them, and be glad. For love is never wasted, love is never lost; love lives on and sees us through sorrow. From the moment love is born it is always with us, keeping us aloft in the flooding and strong in the time of trial. . . .

And so we pray: Receive, O Lord, into your heavenly kingdom the men and women of the great and fabled Screaming Eagles: They must be singing now, in their joy, flying higher than mere men can fly, as flights of angels take them to their rest.

Again, you can't really lessen anyone's sadness in these circumstances, but you can add something to it that will be helpful, that will inspirit. We thought reminding people that their affection was not pointless but in fact had had meaning—those short lives made a difference, their work was peace—

would be something they could sort of take in their hands and look at, ponder, later.

It was at this event that I saw for the first time a change in American grieving styles, and a change in how those who are grieving treated the president. In the 1960s the Kennedys, who had endured much public grieving, had set a style for mourning—straight and stoic, dry eyed, no sobbing and wailing. But in the eighties it started to change and return to the old way. People sobbed in that cold hangar, and embraced. The president and Mrs. Reagan wanted to personally speak to each parent, wife and husband, and they walked down the long rows of mourners, stopping to speak to each. People started to hug him. One young woman showed him a picture. An old black man leaned forward and put his head on Reagan's shoulder, and Reagan put his arms around him.

Now we are used to such things. Now if you forget to hug a president he is sure to grab you, and give you a soulful embrace. But then it was something unusual, something spontaneous and genuinely moving.

A eulogy isn't for the departed and it isn't for you; it is for the grieving people in the pews. Be serious but not somber, and be sincere.

A tribute is for the person being honored, and for those in the audience who want to see him and his work effectively captured, complimented, put into context. Be sincere and gracious.

A toast is for the person or persons being honored; show your affection with sincerity and, if you like, humor.

APPLAUSE

Applause is the physical demonstration of the fact that your audience is listening, thinking and agreeing.

Never wait for applause. Never end a sentence that you think deserves or will get applause and wait for it to begin. Because if it doesn't begin, if they don't start to clap, the silence that follows will be heard by all. It is a silence that talks. It says, "Gee, I thought you'd like that and you don't." It says, "Hey, I thought you'd be easier to manipulate!" It says, "Sorry buddy, keep talking, you haven't won us over."

So: Waiting for applause is like waiting for a compliment. Don't. Just give your speech the best you can and concentrate on what you're saying. Any applause that comes is an unexpected gift.

At the same time, the possibility of applause has to be kept in mind while you're writing your speech.

Suppose you're making a speech about what you feel has become the imbalance between the rights of the states and the rights of the federal government. You will probably note that the tension between those rights was with us from the beginning of the republic, argued out in the Federalist Papers and in Philadelphia in 1776. So it's not new. You might assert that it can be said that the working out of that tension can be seen in our entire history, that the Civil War was a struggle over state and federal rights, that the abortion struggle today is an unresolved struggle between state and federal rights. You might argue that sometime in the past thirty years the facts of the argument changed, that the delicate balance between the states and the federal establishment has been distorted, that it's out of whack, and that for some reasons that were good some things were accepted that were bad. Your position might be that the equal rights of all Americans must be protected and asserted, and in the past thirty years we have so protected and asserted, and this is good. But we allowed the federal establishment to take new powers unto itself in order to do that protecting and asserting, and this has not produced an unalloyed good. It has in fact produced some very bad things indeed.

That's your point of view, and you write it out and stand to speak. Suppose your audience is listening carefully, and agreeing or disagreeing. You make your case, give example after example as evidence that the federal government has taken to itself powers it cannot wield well and does not wield justly.

Suppose now the audience is deeply engaged, and people here and there are beginning to clap.

You must let them. They want to, and they're free Americans. But you have to try to arrange your sentences so that when they clap they can hear you, and you are allowed to finish your thought, or all will end in confusion.

Let's say you intone: "And I will tell you clearly that it is our job now to limit the role of the federal government by pushing it back to its rightful place as ultimate definer and guarantor of our rights, but not the prime asserter of or the great meddler in how we are to live our lives each day."

This isn't good.

The audience starts to clap as you finish saying "limit the role of the federal government." They hear you continue on and stop clapping. Then they hear "back to its rightful place," and applaud again. But still you plow on in an attempt to finish your thought, and end with "how we are to live our lives each day." Then *you* wait for the applause. And it doesn't come. Because you've already fooled them twice. And because your ending's a little lamer than your beginning, which often happens in life, don't you think?

You've got to break your long sentence up into shorter sentences. You're not changing what you're saying, you're only changing how you say it. As in, "I will tell you clearly that it is our job now to limit the role of the federal government." If this gets applause, wait a moment and then continue.

"It is time to push the government back to its rightful place." If this gets applause, wait a moment and then continue.

"For the federal government is the ultimate guarantor of our rights but should not be the first judge of how we live our lives each day."

This arrangement is more likely to allow the audience to applaud at the right time, with everyone able to hear exactly what they're applauding. And you still get to finish your thought, but it doesn't sound like a choppy jumble.

It's an odd thing about applause. We all like it, but it can be as difficult to respond to as a compliment. You think, Yeah? You liked that? But of course you don't say that. The only thing to do with applause is to nod to it, keep doing your job, and occasionally look up, if the applause is sustained, and say, simply, "Thank you." And then get back to work.

GOOD ADVICE FROM A VET

T he columnist Art Buchwald has been a star on the lecture circuit for more than a generation. I asked him recently what he would tell people who are new to speech giving. Actually I said, "Art, are there tricks you can tell me?" He said sure, but they're not tricks, they're just things you do to make it easier for you and nicer for the audience.

First, he said, someone once gave him great advice: "Never change your speech, change your audience."

If you're going to be speaking a lot, create what political professionals call a core speech—a document that includes all the points and stories that these days you want or have to make. For Art, that usually means a speech that includes a lot of funny stories and thoughts about people and things in the news right now.

After you put together such a speech, give it a few times. You'll see what works and what doesn't, what holds your audience's attention and what makes them start sneaking out the back of the room. Keep what works, ditch what doesn't. The core speech is what remains. Keep refining it, keep adding and removing as the days, months or years go by.

SHOW THEM YOU KNOW THEM

Then, said Art, "I write a new top for every speech. I'm talking to the Hewlett-Packard company tomorrow night in San Francisco, so I'll do the first fifteen minutes of the forty-minute speech on computers. All the Internet/computer/E-mail people will be there, and I have several thoughts on it. No one yet has figured out how to pay professional writers for their material when it's published on the Internet, the copyright stuff—so I'll talk about that."

He will make serious points but use humor when he can. He will entertain—"That's what they hired me for."

Buchwald continued, "You have to let the audience know at the beginning that you know about them. Read up on the organization. This is basic. I get material from the company and read it—the yearly report, the annual report, the clippings and press releases. I'll think, as I prepare, Is the computer industry competitive? You better believe it. So if I hear or read in the papers that the Kellogg's corn flakes company is looking for a new computer system and both Hewlett-Packard and IBM want the business, I use it. I find out the name of the Hewlett vice president who's in charge of it, and I give him advice in the speech. I say he should go to Kellogg's and say, 'IBM is full of really nice guys, but they all have venereal disease.'

"When you use the real names of men or women in the organization, that's like gold. They come to you afterwards and say, 'How'd you know so much about our business?' But the people you mention have to be key, important people who are big enough to take a joke.

"If the company has just had a disaster, that's great. I'll say,

'I'm so glad to see you're all here—except for the executives from Frito-Lay.' Gets a big laugh."

ALWAYS DO Q&A

As a matter of fact, though Art didn't say this, a good appearance is often composed of twenty minutes of speech and twenty minutes of questions.

Art said, "The best advice for people who make speeches is: During the question-and-answer period, come up with the best responses you can, and if you're asked something and come up with a funny answer, insert it next time in your speech. ('By the way, I was asked the other day about Mrs. Clinton's hairdos, and I told 'em . . . ')

"The Q-and-A time is the most interesting. This is true for everyone who speaks."

I really agree with this. It's the only time you know you are addressing what's on the audience's mind—because the audience is asking you. Q-and-A is by its nature free flowing and potentially surprising. Topics change quickly, which is a relief: If the audience isn't interested in one question they might be interested in the next. So keep it moving—answer as best you can and point to the next raised hand. Q-and-A is not high wire. In fact, in a way you can't fail. If you have a clever or smart answer to the question the audience is impressed. If you flail about it's not so bad because—how to put it?—people find it kind of interesting when other people flail about. It has the fascination of a clip from a bad movie. And they don't judge you harshly; they're inclined to give you a break because they know you had no time to prepare or think about the question.

By the way, always repeat the question. Chances are the people around the person who asked the question heard it but the rest of the audience didn't. Also, it gives you another five seconds to try to think of an answer.

DON'T BE A JERK

"The thing you don't want to do is try to be part of the gang when you're not and people know you're not. Like a politician who wants to show he knows everyone on the roster and gets the names wrong—'I want to thank my good friend Jack Goo—Goog—Um, Jack, how do you say it, Googenhime?' Or a big foreign policy group hires you to speak at a dinner. Don't impress them with your expertise, make a joke of your lack of it. 'I can't say enough about the Foreign Affairs Council, because I never heard of it before.' "

MEET THEM

"The people who come to lectures are pretty intelligent. If they were dumb they'd be home watching TV. Instead they're out, eager to hear what you have to say. So they're smart. So don't talk down to them.

"They're interested in you. They wouldn't have shown up if they weren't. And they know about you, they've read your books. So in a way it can be intimate.

"Also, the people who invited you to speak and pay you to do it want to touch you. Once before a speech I was at the cocktail party they always have, and I asked, 'Who was the last speaker?' They said, 'Morley Safer.' I said, 'How was he?' They said, 'He

wasn't very good.' I said, 'Whatta ya mean Morley Safer wasn't
very good?' They say, 'He didn't come to the cocktail party.'"

THINK PRACTICAL

"Basically the two things every speaker needs are sound and
light. You should check the sound, go to the mike and speak a
few sentences before you go on and before the audience gets
there. And you should always check to see that you are lit
right—that there's enough light to read your notes on the
podium. If there isn't, go to the manager of the dining room
and tell him what you need."

ONCE YOU'RE REALLY GOOD

"Don't let them tape your speech. It's copyrighted material.
Put it in your contract that they can't tape it. You don't want
people sitting back and watching it if you do this for a living. I
mean, St. Pat's won't hire you if they just heard everything you
said at Temple Emanu-el. And you shouldn't let them have TV
cameras, because it's distracting. But it's right to do a press
interview before or after you speak, if anyone wants it, to be
polite."

GOOD ADVICE FROM ANOTHER VET

U. S. Senator Slade Gorton of the state of Washington has been making speeches in public for forty years. He has a particular way of doing things that works well for him.

This is what he says:

"I gave my first speech in 1947. And I will make a speech tomorrow afternoon to sixty to eighty local businessmen and -women, most of whom are politically sympathetic and many of whom I know. But before the speech my adrenaline level will rise, I will not be able to enjoy my food before I speak, because I will be so distracted by my desire to speak well and make a connection with my audience. You will always get nerves or high adrenaline before you speak—and that's fine, because it has to be like that in order for you to do well.

"There's something I learned unconsciously, and then I was told. If you can possibly do so, speak without having something between you and the audience. Don't have a podium, don't be at a table, don't use a microphone. The more exposed you are to an audience the more connected you will be, the more attention they'll pay, the more likely they will ask you questions. So I even put aside the mike when I can so that it won't be between me and them.

"And you know what? When you speak without a barrier you can say exactly the same thing you'd say behind a podium, and you get twice the impact.

"But to do this you have to know your subject and know exactly what you want to say so you don't have to rely on a text or notes.

"If you find you must rely on a text and therefore need a podium or a table, do it. But then during the question-and-answer time, come from behind the podium and move closer to the audience."

CONSERVE YOURSELF

Don't give your energy away early on. Once I went to speak in the state of Washington at the annual meeting of a homebuilder's association. I landed in Seattle and was picked up by a member of the association for a three-hour drive to a hotel on the western shore. As a rule, it's not a good thing to be picked up by a member of the organization to which you will speak, because they like you, they invited you and are paying you—which means they want to get to know you in the car.

Always ask, if you can, for a car service, which will send a driver who neither knows you nor cares to. In the silence you can work on your speech and notice the landscape, the towns and buildings, and later ask about them and learn.

The young man who picked me up was, unfortunately, bright and gregarious. He began to pepper me with questions. What was Reagan really like? When you write a magazine article, do they tell you what to say?

I have learned from experience that you must nip this in the bud. You want to be polite and friendly, but public speaking is performance art and you don't want to do your material in the car; if you do you'll be tired and flat when you stand before the audience a few hours later. You'll be less good at the thing they're paying you to be good at.

Also, you don't want to be answering questions, but asking them. The one big benefit of spending a lot of time with a representative of the group you're speaking to is that you can learn more about the group, the area, the business, the local political situation, the group's internal politics. You want to be collecting intellectual income, not spending your small treasure.

Anyway, be politely direct with the questioner in the car and tell him or her that while it's a compliment to be asked so many questions, if you answer them now you'll be flat later on, and people will leave disappointed. I told the fellow to ask me three questions and I'd do my best to answer them, and then to let me ask him about things so he could fill me in. Then, I said, I'd have to work on my speech and think about it.

It was fine with him. And I wound up learning great things. People get very candid in cars on long drives.

But don't let anyone tire you before you go on. You'll wind up cheating the people who hired you.

HANDLING STAGE FRIGHT

H ere are things that might help you with stage fright.

The first is to remember: THE NUNS WHO TAUGHT YOU ARE NOT IN THE AUDIENCE.

I have a friend who always thinks they are. And would that they were, for deep in their dark-clad hearts, unknown to you and perhaps themselves, they loved you.

Your audience brings no such intensity. The majority of audiences are composed of a few hundred mildly pleased, mildly bored people who in most cases have to be there. (I disagree with Art Buchwald on this—I think more than half of them *would* rather be home watching TV, and that this has nothing to do with their intelligence but rather their fatigue.) But they're here because it's their job, it's their organization, their business convention, and the boss will notice if they're not.

This shouldn't be disheartening but inspiring. Someone once said that most people just sort of daydream through most days, in a kind of personal fog. Audiences are often foggy, especially if you're the third speaker. But you, the speaker, get to wake them up, get to get them thinking about things they might not otherwise have thought about. And they appreciate when you do this; they receive interesting thoughts and humor as an unexpected gift.

In general, I think audiences just hope a speaker won't be boring and will be entertaining. They're polite to boring speakers, but when someone shows up with good material, they're actually moved.

Anyway, I always think expectations play to the speaker's advantage.

DON'T WORRY ABOUT BEING SMOOTH AND SLICK

They're Americans, they've seen smooth and slick, they're not impressed. A winning eagerness, a surprising awkwardness, an ingenuous lack of perfection—these are endearing things to see in a successful person. Which is what you are by definition or they wouldn't have asked you to speak. If I saw a candidate or a business leader speak and they were perfect, I'd tell them: "Be less perfect. It's tough enough on some of your audience that you've done so well in life."

GO INTO THE ROOM

Go into the room where you'll speak before the audience gets there and go up to the podium. Look out at the room. Get used to its size. Lean into the mike and speak. Say a few words, hear your voice. This will get you acclimated. It will also give you a sense, when you're introduced and take the podium, that you've been here before and nothing terrible happened.

It's also a way to find out if the mike doesn't work or you need a light on the podium. Tell whoever is running the event what you need and they'll be eager to help you. They want everything to work and you to be good.

MAKE FRIENDS WITH THE AUDIENCE

Once you're at the event be friendly to people, show respect. If you're pumped or nervous it will help you get rid of excess energy or tension. If there's one of those cocktail things before lunch or dinner, go to it. Meet people, thank them for inviting you. You're converting them from stranger to new friend, and it's easier to speak to friends. Also, it shows you appreciate their inviting you; nausea can make you forget it's an honor, but it is.

If there's one particular person you're nervous about—a board member who is an old enemy, or the wife of the president of the organization, who happens to remember you as the guy who didn't marry her twenty years ago—make a beeline to him or her and say hello, talk, perhaps grovel. Then later when you stand to speak and they're watching you with their beady eyes it'll be okay, the pressure won't be so great, because you've already "made a speech" to them.

CREATE YOUR OWN POSSE

This one always works. If you're really nervous when you arrive, go up to all the strangers seated at the big round white tables in the ballroom where you'll speak. Introduce yourself, thank them for coming. They'll be surprised by your graciousness, and touched by it. And you can forget your woes in the ensuing conversation. Someone is sure to tell you their cousin went to your college. You'll ask, deadpan, "Did he . . . turn out okay?' They'll deadpan, 'Better than we expected.'

I not only shake hands and thank everybody, I tell them how nervous I am. Then I ask for their help. I tell them I fear that fear will so constrict my throat that I won't be able to speak. They usually say things like, "That won't happen," or "That's the way I feel when I have to speak." Then I deputize them. I tell them that if I lose my voice I want one of them to help by creating a diversion.

How, they ask.

Well, I say, just sort of . . . say something.

"I'll ask a question," one of them will say. Then someone will volunteer to sing. Then someone will say his wife will sing "The Star-Spangled Banner." I say that sounds good to me. People sometimes get into it. Sometimes when I'm making the speech and a joke falls flat I'll make an aside to them—"Joe at table two, get ready."

Anyway, this always helps me. It's good to have a little platoon.

If you can't be on the floor talking to people at tables, talk to the people on the dais. Go down the line, saying hello to everyone. It's surprising how many people don't do this. But the other dais-hostages always appreciate it.

IF YOU REALLY HAVE TO, BE A COMPLETE COWARD

If you're still on the sick edge of terror it may make you feel better to set up an excuse for failure in advance. Turn to the person on your right on the dais and say, "Gee, my brain tumor's really acting up today." This not only gives you an excuse, it's a real icebreaker.

SOME ADVICE FOR THE PERVERSE

As I said, I never made a speech until I was forty. A few hundred speeches later the fear hasn't lessened. But a thing that has helped me is realizing that if I fail utterly, if I faint, babble or spew, if people walk out flinging the heavy linen napkins onto the big round tables in disgust . . . my life continues as good as it was. Better. Because fewer people will ask me to speak. So flopping would be good for me.

The minute I remember this I don't flop.

You Can Break Every Rule and Do Fine

MOTHER TERESA
KNOCKS 'EM OUT

N ow that I have spoken of things to keep in mind as you write and give a speech, I want to talk about somebody who broke almost all the rules and still gave a speech that was deeply memorable and enormously powerful. I do this to inspire you: Ultimately your own way is the best way, and mistakes are not always mistakes.

On February 3, 1994, Mother Teresa came to Washington and gave a speech that left the entire audience dazzled and part of it dismayed—including a United States senator who turned to his wife after Mother Teresa concluded and said, "Is my jaw up yet?"

It was the annual National Prayer Breakfast at the Hilton Hotel and three thousand people were there, including most of official Washington. The breakfast is always an interesting and unusual gathering in the capital in that it is informed by an unspoken goodwill and because famous people, usually political figures, are invited to talk about what they rarely talk about in public: their understanding of God, their pursuit of Him, His place in their lives. The assumption is that they will speak candidly, and from what I've seen they pretty much do. I have attended three of the breakfasts over the years and been touched by the candor and also the sweetness of much of what I heard. (I wish I'd been at the one back in the seventies when the Catholic bishop Fulton J. Sheen began his remarks with a mock-stern, "Fellow sinners," and turned to President Carter and said, "And that means you, too." Carter and the audience roared.)

By tradition the president of the United States and the first lady always attend, and on this day in 1994 Bill and Hillary Clinton were up there on the dais, as were the vice president and Mrs. Gore and a dozen other important people, senators and Supreme Court justices.

The busy ballroom hummed. Everyone seemed happy to be there, they were friendly and talkative—it was 7:30 in the morning and people had the undefended, approachable look morning sleepiness can give. There was an air of excitement and anticipation: An appearance by Mother Teresa was always an event, for she was not only a saint but a very old one who would not be with us forever.

When I saw her on television or in the papers I always thought of Malcolm Muggeridge, who journeyed to Calcutta to interview her for the BBC in 1969 and who reported the following. His interview with Mother Teresa had been difficult to arrange and would take place in Calcutta's Home for the Dying, a dimly lit cavern in which filming would be, according to the experienced cameraman, quite impossible. Nonetheless it would be their only chance to see the reluctant nun in her habitat, and so they gave it a go and hoped. Later in London the film was developed to reveal that the room was lit, beautifully and fully, by a radiant light. Where did it come from? No one knew. The cameraman insisted it could not happen as it happened. Muggeridge, a renowned intellectual and yet also an intelligent man, immediately thought: God did this. He wrote of the incident in his book *Something Beautiful for God,* the best-seller that introduced Mother Teresa to the West, which began to give so generously to her order that its work was able to spread across the globe. What he wrote was, "I myself am absolutely convinced that the technically unaccountable light is, in fact, the Kindly Light [Cardinal] Newman refers to.... Mother Teresa's Home for the Dying is overflowing with love.... This love is luminous, like the halos artists have seen and made visible round the heads of the saints. I find it not at all surprising that the luminosity should register on a photographic film."

And now here she was—or rather here we were, at 7:45 A.M., waiting. She was not on the dais, presumably because you cannot ask a saint to sit around fidgeting with breakfast rolls and talking NAFTA. That is what presidents are for. And Mr. Clinton did his part with his usual friendliness, listening attentively and applauding warmly as the first speakers rose to welcome the crowd.

Then Mother Teresa was introduced and came from behind a parted curtain to walk to the podium. She was small and moved slowly, hunched forward slightly as those with osteoporosis often are. She wore a white, blue-edged, floor-length habit and looked weathered, frail and tough as wire.

As she stepped up onto a little platform that had been placed beneath the podium there was great applause. She nodded at it. Then she took her speech in her hand and began to read from it in a soft singsong voice:

Make us worthy, Lord, to serve our fellow men throughout the
world who live and die in poverty and hunger. Give them
through our hands this day their daily bread, and by our understanding love, give peace and joy.

No thank you, no smile. She just stood there holding the
speech and looking down at it. She didn't look up or make eye
contact, nor did she gesture with her hands.

For the next twenty-five minutes she never said anything
designed to elicit applause. She just read, and appeared sometimes to be ad-libbing from, her text.

She spoke of God, of love, of families, and told us we must
love each other and care for each other. As she spoke I looked
around. There were three thousand people in the room, with
a plate before each of cool scrambled eggs and warm fruit.
They did not eat, but listened, leaning forward in an attitude
of unconscious communion. The audience was composed of
liberal Democrats, conservative Republicans and moderates of
all persuasion. Perhaps half were Christian members of the
prayer breakfast movement, some quite seriously devout and
some less so—there's a bit of this-world networking that goes
on. The other half was a mix—Muslims, Jews, searchers, agnos-
tics and atheists, reporters and bureaucrats, waiters and diplo-
mats. A good-natured and attentive mix. And they all loved
her.

But as the speech continued it became more pointed. Since
Christ, she said, gave up everything to do his Father's will, so
must we be willing to give up everything to do God's will:

If we are not willing to give whatever it takes to do good to one
another, sin is still in us. That is why we, too, must give to each
other until it hurts. It is not enough for us to say, "I love God." I

also have to love my neighbor. St. John said that you are a liar if you say you love God and you don't love your neighbor. How can you love God, whom you do not see, if you do not love your neighbor, whom you see, whom you touch, with whom you live? And so it is very important for us to realize that love, to be true, has to hurt. I must be willing to give whatever it takes not to harm other people, and, in fact, to do good to them. . . . Otherwise, there is no true love in me, and I bring injustice, not peace, to those around me.

To some in the crowd these words constituted a strong and moving admonition. To some they were pretty pieties. But to some, her words seemed to be addressing the doctrine of *solo fide*, faith alone. The Catholic Church teaches that faith without works is not enough. Protestantism teaches that faith alone is sufficient for salvation. In my sincere but deservedly humble view this is a frustrating disagreement because it is marked most by a kind of willful misunderstanding—but it is a real one, and goes to the heart of resistance to Christian reunification.

So things were getting interesting. And people in the audience were starting to look at each other, eyebrows up.

Then she spoke of how, when Jesus was dying on the cross, he said, "I thirst." He was thirsting, she said, and is thirsting, for our love. And we are all like this, we all thirst.

I can never forget the experience I had in the sitting room [of an American nursing home] where they kept all these old parents of sons and daughters who had just put them into an institution and forgotten them, maybe. I saw that in that home, these old people had everything—good food, comfortable place, television, everything—but everyone was looking toward the door. And I did not see a single one with a smile on their face. I turned to a sister and I asked, "Why do these people who have every comfort here, they are looking toward the door? Why are they not smiling? I'm so used to seeing the smiles on our people. Even the dying ones smile." And Sister said, "This is the way it is nearly every day. They are expecting, they are hoping that the son or the daughter will come to visit them. They are hurt because they are forgotten." And see, this neglect to love brings spiritual poverty. Maybe in our own family we have some-body who is feeling lonely, who is feeling sick, who is feeling wor-ried. Are we there? Are we willing to give until it hurts in order to be with our family, or do we put our interests first?

Those are challenging words, and would be experienced as such by an audience dominated by middle-aged people some of whom haven't talked to Mom and Pop in a while, or didn't talk enough when Mom and Pop were here. It was the kind of truth that makes people shift a little in their seats, or shift psy-chically to other thoughts.

Then came this:

In the families of the West, she said, it is not unusual that "[the] father and the mother are so busy they have no time for their children, or perhaps they are not even married or have given up on their marriage. So the children go to the streets and get involved in drugs and other things." This is tragic, she said, for it is within the child that the love and peace of adult-hood begin, therefore it is within the family that love and peace must reign.

There was a bit more shifting now, for an audience com-posed of humans is an audience composed of sinners, and an audience dominated by busy boomer parents is composed of veterans of sin.

She continued, "But I feel that the greatest destroyer of peace today is abortion, because Jesus said, 'If you receive a little child, you receive me.' So every abortion is the denial of receiving Jesus, the neglect of receiving Jesus."

Well, silence. Cool deep silence in the cool round cavern for just about 1.3 seconds. And then applause started on the right-hand side of the room, and spread, and deepened, and now the room was swept with people applauding, and they would not stop for what I believe was five or six minutes. As they clapped they began to stand, in another wave from the right of the room to the center and the left.

But not everyone applauded. The president and first lady, seated within a few feet of Mother Teresa on the dais, were not applauding. Nor were the vice president and Mrs. Gore. They looked like seated statues at Madame Tussaud's. They glistened in the lights and moved not a muscle, looking at the speaker in a determinedly semi-pleasant way.

I was applauding at my table, and most of my tablemates were standing, and I turned to look at what the friendly and intelligent woman to my right was doing. We had had a nice conversation before the speaking began. She was a lawyer, the wife of a member of the Clinton administration, a modern and attractive blond-haired woman in her late forties or early fifties.

She was not applauding. She was staring straight ahead, impassively, if you can call white lips and a stricken expression impassive.

Now, Mother Teresa is not perhaps schooled in the ways of world capitals and perhaps did not know that having said her piece and won the moment she was supposed to go back to the airier, less dramatic assertions on which we all agree.

Instead she said this:

[Abortion] is really a war against the child, and I hate the killing
of the innocent child, murder by the mother herself. And if we
accept that the mother can kill even her own child, how can we
tell other people not to kill one another? How do we persuade a
woman not to have an abortion? As always, we must persuade
her with love. . . . The father of that child, however, must also
give until it hurts. By abortion, the mother does not learn to
live, but kills even her own child to solve her problem. And by
abortion, the father is taught that he does not have to take any
responsibility at all for the child he has brought into that world.
So that father is likely to put other women into the same trouble. So abortion just leads to more abortion.

Any country that accepts abortion is not teaching its people to
love one another but to use any violence to get what they want.
This is why the greatest destroyer of love and peace is abortion.

Again applause, and I looked once more to the woman on
my right. As the applause spread she sat back in her chair and
folded her hands on her lap. Then she briskly reached for her
purse and took out a notepad. She took out a slim gold pen. It
gleamed in the ballroom lights. She started writing down
words.

I couldn't resist, I peered as un-obviously as I could to see
what she was writing. "Shop Rite," it said on the hospital-white
pad. "Cleaners."

She was making a To Do list. That was how she detached
from the moment. She did not like what she had just heard
but she couldn't walk out, couldn't boo, so she made a little
list of things to do.

I looked toward the dais. Hillary Clinton was still staring
straight ahead, unmoving. I imagined her looking at my table-
mate and yelling over, "Don't forget the Tide."

Mother Teresa now spoke of fighting abortion with adoption, of telling hospitals and police stations and frightened young girls, "Please don't kill the child. I want the child. Give me the child. I'm willing to accept any child who would be aborted and to give that child to a married couple who will love the child and be loved by the child."

Later I was to remember this part as Mother Teresa's carpet bombing. Then she dropped the big one:

I know that couples have to plan their family, and for that there is natural family planning. The way to plan the family is natural family planning, not contraception. In destroying the power of giving life or loving through contraception, a husband or wife is doing something to self. This turns the attention to self, and so it destroys the gift of love in him and her. In loving, the husband and wife must turn the attention to each other, as happens in natural family planning, and not to self, as happens in contraception. Once that living love is destroyed by contraception, abortion follows very easily. That's why I never give a child to a family that has used contraception, because if the mother has destroyed the power of loving, how will she love my child?

It was at this point that the senator turned to his wife and asked if his jaw was still up.

It was something, the silence and surprise with which her words were received. Perhaps she didn't know that we don't talk about birth control in speeches in America. Perhaps she didn't know, or care, that her words were, as they say, not "healing" but "divisive," dividing not only Protestant from Catholic but Catholic from Catholic. It was all so unhappily unadorned, explicit, impolitic. And it was wonderful, like a big fresh drink of water, bracing in its directness and its uncompromising tone.

And of course it was startling too, as if someone had spoken in favor of the Volstead Act. And indeed the Clintons and Gores looked, by the end, as if they'd heard someone promise to outlaw Merlot.

Mother Teresa seemed neither to notice nor care. She finished her speech to a standing ovation and left as she had entered, silently, through a parted curtain, in a flash of blue and white.

Her speech was a great success in that it was clear and strong, seriously meant, seriously stated, seriously argued and seriously received. She spoke with a complete indifference to the conventions of speech giving, not only in her presentation—reading the text as if she were reading some dry old document aloud, rarely looking up, rarely using her voice to emphasize, rarely using inflection, expression or gesturing—but in her message. She softened nothing, did not deflect division but defined it. She came with a sword.

She could do this, of course, because she had and has a natural and known authority. She has the standing of a saint.

May you pursue and achieve such standing as you think and work and write and speak.

SUMMING UP

I was going to end with the Mother Teresa story but my editor had a better idea: "Tell 'em what you told 'em," sum up the suggestions to keep in mind as you prepare your speech.

First, *be not afraid.* Whatever your fears about writing and speaking, the bad things you imagine are not likely to happen. And if they do, you'll survive. Every great speaker in history has flopped somewhere along the way, most of them more than once. So relax. It's only a speech.

Second, as you write you must *think logically about the case you're making, and make it.* Take notes about the points you want to cover and put them in order. Try to imagine your speech being reduced to a headline—WILSON SAYS CIVIL RIGHTS BILL NECESSARY, or whatever. Write with the headline in mind. It will help keep you focused.

Third, *your style shouldn't be taller than you are.* Don't be self-consciously stentorian, don't imitate the high oratory of past presidents and generals. Say it the way you'd say it if you were speaking, with concentration and respect, to a friend. Your own style will emerge with time as you write and speak.

Fourth, remember that *the most moving thing in a speech is always the logic*—the case you are making, the problem you are outlining, the remedy you believe in and support. Don't try to move people by manipulating them with phony emotionalism or faux poetry. If you make your case well and clearly and with some wit and feeling, you just may find that you've moved your audience to tears. But never try to make them cry, try to help them think.

Fifth, that reminds me: *Use humor when you can.* Why? Because it makes people laugh. No one ever left a speech saying, "He was too witty," or "I hated the way she made me laugh out loud."

Sixth, *give your speech before you give it.* Read a draft or two aloud to friends or family. This is where you'll discover such problems as unpronounceable words, undeliverable sentences and unpursuasive arguments.

And seventh, *use your own gestures, respect your own quirks.* There's a whole industry out there that exists to tell people how to move their hands and faces when they're speaking in public. It's one of the reasons so many politicians and TV journalists sound alike and gesture alike: They've all been trained, often by the same professionals. I would advise you not to worry too much about presentation, and not to be eager to sound and move like everyone else. You don't have to be smooth; your audience is composed of Americans, and they've seen smooth. Instead, be you. They haven't seen that yet.

A NOTE TO WRITERS

John Gregory Dunne once called writing "intellectual pipe laying." He meant that it is hard work that you do not with your back but with your brain, spirit and soul. Pipe layers rest between bursts of activity, and so must you.

Take walks. Work for a few hours and then go for a walk, amble along and look at the trees or the stores or the people or the squirrels. This will not only give you new things to daydream about—and daydreaming is important, for it is your mind unclenching and yielding up connections and images that may be useful to you—but will get the circulation going in your legs again.

I think the working nap is a necessary luxury. Sometimes when you've been working hard for a few hours your brain really fires up and barrels, but sometimes it just tires and goes flat. If you start flatlining, take a break, lie down, and let your brain go to sleep for forty-five minutes or so. This is restorative. It's replenishing. And you may find that in the brief space between being awake and being asleep your brain free-associates to a degree that can prove helpful.

A small example. A while back I was working on a short essay for *Time* magazine and it just wasn't working. Whatever I had to say was eluding me. I kept trying to stay on the big river but kept getting diverted down shallow streams. Where I'd get stuck. So I went to lie down. The day before I had been browsing in a jewelry store, and had gone on to visit a friend in a Manhattan business office. As I fell asleep my mind played: I was standing in the lobby of the skyscraper about to press the round brass elevator button when I saw that it was a beautiful, gleaming earring. I thought, How interesting to find a jewel in such a place.

I woke up inspired, for my brain was telling me that in spite of my difficulties with the essay it was still capable of saying something truthful and interesting today. (The friend I had visited is indeed a gem.) I rewrote the essay, which advised Bob Dole to go home to Kansas and wage his presidential campaign from his old front porch. The essay went fine, the Dole campaign ignored my advice and didn't. That'll learn 'em.

Reading is another necessary luxury. William Safire once told a budding writer, "Never feel guilty about reading, it's what you do to do your job." Reading is the collecting of intellectual income; writing is the spending of it. You need to read to write, you need to take in other people's words and thoughts and images. If you want to be a good conversationalist you must both talk and listen; if you want to be a good writer you must both write and read.

The writer Annie Dillard once warned, however, that you must watch what you read when you're writing, for other people's voices and even subject matter come into your head and change your work, affect it in ways that can be subtle and of which you're unaware. So when you're working on something important to you, read good writers. Let their excellence seep in. When I was a speechwriter I spent a lot of time reading the great speeches of past presidents. I don't know how it helped me but it did. I think their authority seeped in.

Look, for inspiration, to the excellence of other people.

INDEX